THE QUIET MIND

THE
QUIET MIND

JOHN E. COLEMAN

PARIYATTI PRESS
ONALASKA, WASHINGTON

Pariyatti Press
867 Larmon Road
Onalaska, WA 98570, USA

❋

First Edition 1971, Rider & Company, London
First American Edition 1971, Harper and Row, New York

© 1971, 2000 by John E. Coleman

Second Edition, 2000

Published by Pariyatti Press, 2000.

ISBN-10 1-928706-06-1

ISBN 978-1-928706-06-9 (Print) 2012

ISBN 978-1-928706-55-7 (Ebook-PDF) 2011

09 08 07 06 05 04 03 02 01   5 4 3 2 1

Library of Congress Cataloging-in-Publication Data
Coleman, John E., 1930-
  The quiet mind / John E. Coleman.-- 2nd ed.
    p. cm.
  ISBN 1-928706-06-1 (pbk.)
   1. Meditation. 2. Peace of mind--Religious aspects--Buddhism. 3.
Buddhism--Doctrines. 4. Parapsychology. 5. Coleman, John E., 1930- I. Title.
BL627 .C65 2000
294.3'44--dc21
                                                    00-056659

Printed in the United States of America

CONTENTS

LIST OF ILLUSTRATIONS AND MAPS

Publisher's Preface

Nearly thirty years have passed since the first edition of *The Quiet Mind* appeared in print. Many of the individuals encountered in the author's search are no longer with us. Why then reissue this book, when many of its potential readers were not even born at the time of the events portrayed? The search for a quiet mind is a universal search. The tools for the search are universal tools, and the answers are universal answers.

Since this book was originally published, there seems to have been a flood tide of interest in "the search." *The Quiet Mind* remains a testament to this search, and offers the hope and the inspiration that the goal can be reached.

This second edition expands on the original edition with the addition of a postscript, which tells the story of the author's experience since the events in the book, and describes how the tools for finding a "quiet mind" have spread to the West since the first edition.

A note on terminology

Many of the terms used by the author come from the rich complex of languages of the Indian subcontinent. Pāli is used in the Theravādin, or southern Buddhist tradition of the author's primary teachers. For readability however, the author has used the more familiar Sanskrit forms for words such as *karma*, rather than the Pāli *kamma*, and *nirvana* rather than the Pāli *nibbāna*. Less common words, such as *sīla*, *anattā*, and *dukkha* have been left in Pāli. When quoting teachers directly, the original Pāli language has been left unchanged.

Also to be noted are two distinct uses of the phrase "transcendental meditation." When used to refer specifically to the technique taught by Maharishi Mahesh Yogi, the words are capitalized; when used to refer in general to meditation whose goal is to "transcend" ordinary reality, the phrase is left in small letters.

Since the writing of *The Quiet Mind*, the name of Burma has changed to Myanmar, and its capital, formerly Rangoon, is now known as Yangon. The original usages have not been changed for this edition.

Introduction

A Question of Conflict

IN all life there is conflict. A plant has to thrust its way through the soil to reach daylight, a newborn baby has to yell to fill its lungs with oxygen. A wild animal must kill to eat or go hungry: either way there is conflict for the animal. As human beings we meet it every day and in everything we do, for conflict is part of living.

And as humans we are very accomplished at providing ourselves with various forms of relaxation or diversion to help us ease up on the pressure.

Whatever form our relaxation takes we ask one of two things from it. If life has been hectic we want peace and quiet, if our routine is dull and uneventful we demand to be "taken out of ourselves." We don't have to look far to satisfy these commonplace requirements, and we are not overanxious to notice just how temporary are their revitalizing effects.

What many people today want to know, and what I was determined to find out, is: can there be a condition, a pool of quiet where the active, restless mind can completely switch off, opt out of the conflict, and still remain purposeful, wholesome, communicative and creative?

In this report I have recorded my search for this condition. I have recalled the circumstances which set me off on the search, traced its progress and described its results.

Part of the mystery of the Far East lies in the fact that in that part of the world the kind of questions to which I wanted answers do not bring raised eyebrows and impatient protests of "nonsense." Meditation, strange religious practices designed to free the mind, even faith in occult powers which throw light on the more obscure mental processes, are not dismissed as unfruitful areas of research.

On the contrary, I found the outlook of the people and their approach to daily life provided just the right atmosphere for my search and, probably because of the novelty of a Westerner showing an interest, many wise and respected people helped.

Not only was the atmosphere right and the people helpful, I had plenty of opportunity to follow my inquiries. My business in the Far East was "import-export" or, rather, that was the name it went under. I was employed as an espionage agent by the U.S. Central Intelligence Agency.

While stationed in Bangkok under my "business" cover I was assigned to the Thai Ministry of the Interior as an advisor to the Thai Police Department on national security and antisubversive matters. My duties brought me into close contact with a wide range of people including senior government officials, members of royalty, civic leaders, educators, the social elite, religious leaders, professional and business people, labourers and peasants. Altogether a pretty representative section of the community, which gave me an excellent and valuable insight into Thai life and mentality.

And some of my duties involved considerable travel both inside Thailand and throughout the Far East and South East Asia, with the occasional trip to Washington for training and debriefing.

In 1957 an Army *coup d'etat* resulted in the overthrow of the Prime Minister and his Government and the exile of the police chief, a powerful political figure at the time, with whom I was working closely. The Army was determined to undermine the influence of the Police Department and directed a newspaper campaign against the activities of the C.I.A., exposing its operations to the public. Being engaged in some delicate activities at the time and being exposed as a U.S. Intelligence agent to the world press contributed eventually to my being placed on the retired list—a spy put out in the cold.

But by this time my investigator's instincts were carrying me along very different paths from my accustomed counterespionage work. Exciting and adventurous though the job was to a young bachelor, I now found myself on to something infinitely more satisfying. Perhaps with the prospect of marriage and a family to look after it was just as well, for the life of a spy working at all hours, often away from home for weeks on end and sometimes in highly dangerous circumstances is not exactly conducive to good family relations.

My twelve years with C.I.A. brought me into close contact with most of the non-Communist peoples of the world. In those hectic and action packed years I had assignments at one time or another in many capitals and major centers, not all of them "trouble spots." And one of the advantages of living out of a suitcase is that you get to know many different people, different races with different political and social viewpoints, different personalities. It is one of the compensations for a way of life that is often uncomfortable and always unsettled.

I graduated from it with a fairly extensive knowledge of people in all their shapes and sizes, outlooks, shades of opinion, and with a feeling for the problems and anxieties most of the world's populations face. It added impetus and meaning to my search for the quiet mind to know that, if the results were successful, a great many people could benefit.

❀

Although much of the investigation involved inquiry into ancient Eastern religious and philosophical doctrines, I have deliberately left out any heavy and detailed description which I felt was outside the scope of this particular book. There are plenty of more scholarly works on the market which will satisfy the reader's thirst for further knowledge.

Wherever necessary I have given brief outlines, but only brief, of doctrines in order to help the reader grasp the relevance of the situations and the reasons for the conclusions I drew. Having this background the reader will more readily be able to relate the ultimate experience of mystic meditation with the actions necessary to induce it. But my interpretations of religious doctrines, I must emphasize, are strictly personal.

I hope readers will read the account that follows for pleasure, not as a study. If I made an error at all it was in regarding the matter too seriously, scrutinizing the various facets of it too closely. I don't mean this flippantly. Paradoxical though it may seem the intellect can be a bar to success and a too intellectual approach can lead one away from achieving this peace that surpasses all understanding, rather than nearer.

I found that once the intellectual approach was abandoned and

I settled down seriously to the task of intuitive meditation complete understanding followed because the search itself had stopped. This rare and even unique understanding is complete and goes beyond all the knowledge one can gain in a lifetime of intellectual study.

This account, then, is not meant to be an academic thesis. It is simply the story of a search, the personal experiences and the discoveries which led one man to a state of mind which has increased the joy of living and the ability to cope effectively with life's problems. As such, I think many will find it entertaining and I hope some may find it of value.

Meditation has become a vogue in recent years—or at least enjoyed some popular notoriety since the visitations of certain Eastern mystics to the West. I have heard people express concern that the pursuit and attainment of the mysterious "transcendental" state might leave them in a "vegetable" condition mentally or put them on an intellectually supramundane plane where they fear they will float above and beyond ordinary worldly existence. They fear that, once having experienced it, they will no longer enjoy normal pleasures, including the masochistic sufferings of life.

Fears like these are totally groundless. The fruits of meditation, when it is truly achieved, give one a new lease on life, redouble an individual's capacity for vigorous and creative action by eliminating all obsession with the pursuit of pleasure or the evasion of pain, and indeed promote the full enjoyment of life with all its good and bad, its beauty and ugliness. It permits one to act instead of constantly reacting. It frees the mind from the eternal conflict of the opposites. Even more, it enhances one's feelings of compassion so that this freedom cannot be used to the detriment of others and that alone is no small virtue in today's environment.

Every subject has its own peculiar jargon and it is all too easy for a writer to slip in strange sounding words or phrases that will pass completely over the heads of most of his readers. I have used words like *satori, nirvana* and *anicca* only when no English word would do, and they are all explained as the story unfolds.

My intention all along has been to express the subject matter in as direct and simple a fashion as possible and bring it right down from the esoteric to the mundane—for the heart of meditation is itself so simple as to go beyond the comprehension of a too highly intellectual approach. A full study of Buddhism or any other Eastern philosophy will soon get the student entangled in a mass of technical detail with a weird and wonderful vocabulary of its own which in the end might help him to master his subject. But this is not my intention.

One other point: although Eastern religious thoughts and teachings are spotlighted more than others in this account it does not follow that a person seeking the quiet mind state for himself must abandon his existing religious convictions and turn to Buddhism. The goal is to transcend the teachings of others and experience directly the liberation which can only come from within.

In my own case I found the original teachings of Buddha—before they were corrupted, as I believe they have been, by the ignorance and vanity of his followers down the centuries—provided a clearer and more direct avenue to this liberation than any of the other religions into which I inquired. No doubt the others have produced their saints and enlightened ones but the correct application of Buddhist thought seems to me the simplest and most direct to reach what I was aiming for and what, I believe, many are aiming for today.

In the last analysis it is freedom from any form of prescribed doctrinal cult that brings truth and a quiet mind, not the dependence upon a faith that promises comfort.

JOHN E. COLEMAN
1971

1

Hypnosis or Something Else?

I WAS lying on a straw mat on the stone floor of a temple in Bangkok. It was cool. There was no sound. I was flat on my back trying to feel relaxed and succeeding.

Suddenly my right arm began to lift involuntarily. It moved upward very slowly and gently until it was stretching straight out from my body and pointing to the domed, ornate ceiling. It hung there for a few moments, then lowered itself to the floor.

The effect must have been creepy. The only light in the place came from the narrow windows whose wooden shutters were opened to the blue sky. There was complete silence.

Worse was to come. Without any warning my other arm began to stir and it, too, rose gradually to an upright position and then lowered. After a minute or two my left leg rose up to a vertical position, then my right leg. Then an arm went up and both legs came down, then both legs and both arms moved up and down together.

I am assured this description of my actions is accurate, ridiculous though it sounds. To an onlooker the scene must have verged on the absurd. And I know I would have felt thoroughly embarrassed—or laughed outright at my own comic antics—if I had been remotely aware of what was happening.

After all, a senior representative of a foreign government with a civil servant's fair share of natural inhibitions giving this kind of performance in a public place is not really what the Thais expected of visitors to their country.

But in fact the odd thing was that I had absolutely no idea at all that anything unusual was taking place.

Then I heard the chuckles that were coming from the other end of the temple....

❉

But let me begin at the beginning. I had heard of meditation, hypnosis, the hallucinatory effects of some drugs like LSD, extra-sensory perception and the like. And I was about as interested or disinterested as any average person. The subject had about as much appeal for me as interplanetary travel, which I can read about with some fascination and then leave strictly to the experts.

Basically I was never a particularly religious man, although I hope I know how to respect the beliefs of those who are, and you could count on your fingers and toes the number of times I've actually worshipped inside a church.

But wherever my job has taken me I have always made a practice of soaking up local atmosphere and learning as much as I could about the indigenous habits and customs and the religious peculiarities of the natives. It became something of a self-imposed obligation with me, for I realized I was more fortunate than most travelers in that my globe-trotting was all done "on the State"—and there are not many countries to which Washington has not sent me, and paid my expenses, on one mission or another. I felt always that it would be somehow less than grateful if I did not make the most of the opportunities this way of life presented.

And here I was on an assignment in Bangkok, magic sounding capital of Thailand, the Technicolor "King and I" country, land of legendary beauty known, if at all in the West, for its rice, its rattan palms, its teak forests, its pineapples, custard apples, bread fruits and mango, its flourishing mineral industry pouring tin, gold, silver, rubies, sapphires, copper and iron into a growing national economy. And celebrated also for its 16,000 temples, for Thailand is a seat of Buddhist learning and philosophy which is followed by no less than a third of the entire world population.

I was on a three-year posting as an advisor on security matters to the Thai Government. I lived in a large house in the residential part of the city and had made a number of friends in the short time I had been there. I had an office near the Government buildings and one of my frequent callers was a colonel of the Thai police named Vasit, a man about my own age.

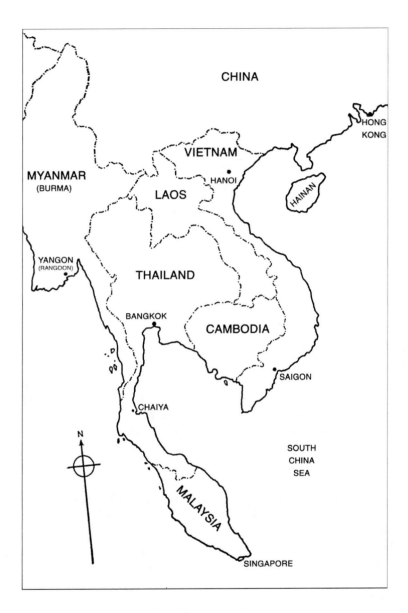

MAP 1 SOUTHEAST ASIA

As the months went by we became firm friends and one day he invited me to attend a meeting of a psychical research group.

In the West we would think twice about accepting this kind of invitation but the occult plays a normal part of everyday religion in the East and I knew there was nothing strange in the suggestion. It was a compliment, in fact, and meant that I was becoming more and more accepted by the people among whom I was living.

Vasit told me the group, composed mainly of medical and religious people, were going to investigate the case of a young Thai boy who had displayed various extrasensory perception abilities under hypnosis.

According to Buddhist doctrine the mind is capable of many—to us quite astonishing—extrasensory phenomena at various stages of deep meditation and I will give some interesting examples of this later in my narrative. I agreed to go along, partly because hypnotism to me was strictly a stage entertainment and I would welcome the break from routine which the experience would afford, and partly through sheer curiosity and a desire to observe at close quarters the kind of people who would give up their time to consider, in all seriousness, a boy playing tricks.

I was in for a surprise. When Vasit and I reached the Wat Magut (Wat means temple) we were greeted by a small gathering of rather learned looking professional people and a handful of holymen smiling and chatting amiably together, exactly as though this was a college common room and they were about to go in to a lecture.

I was introduced to an obstetrician, an anesthetist, a dentist, a psychiatrist, all of whom told me that in their professional capacities they had used hypnotism on their patients and they were interested to compare the hypnotic states with the trancelike states found in meditation. I was impressed by the earnestness with which they discussed the subject.

The boy was then introduced to the assembly. He was a shy, good-looking youngster of about 12 and I noticed at once how alert and bright-eyed he was, though at the same time understandably ill at ease being the center of so much grown up attention.

The boy's most striking performance was with the blackboard test. His eyes were covered with cotton pads and sealed with adhesive tape. He was put into a hypnotic state and led behind an easel on which an ordinary school blackboard was placed. Various members of the group in turn chalked words on the front of the board, while the boy, without any hesitation, and without any kind of guidance or preknowledge of the words to be used, repeated exactly the same words in chalk on the back. The lad was using his mind to receive mental messages from the minds of those who were chalking up the words. To me the whole scene was baffling.

We tested his powers of concentration with unfamiliar words in his own language, then with other languages including English, Chinese and Russian. In every case he reproduced on his side of the blackboard what we had written on the front.

I concluded that the boy would make a small fortune for himself with such a demonstration back home, but of course I was careful not to show any skepticism. How did he do it? Were his senses so sharp that he could remember accurately the sound sequences made by the movements of the chalk on the opposite side of the blackboard? To the gathering of Buddhist scholars present it was a clear demonstration of thought transference while the subject was under deep hypnosis—and in all conscience I could come up with no better explanation.

When the show was over I asked if I might attend further meetings and was readily accepted, as genuinely interested foreigners always are by the friendly Thais. At the next meeting I was even more impressed, this time by several doctors who performed a series of demonstrations to show the value of hypnosis in the medical profession.

An obstetrician produced a young woman in the late stages of pregnancy and gave a talk on how hypnosis was used in teaching the girl to condition herself for a painless childbirth, a practice now fairly common in the West.

More dramatically, a dentist brought along a rather alarmed looking patient with a jaw which ached with obvious violence, placed him under hypnosis and extracted the offending tooth without drugs and apparently without pain. Of course it was possible that the dentist, had he wished to pull the wool over our eyes, could have pumped sufficient novocaine into the poor fellow's gums earlier to see him through the ordeal.

It was clear I would not be allowed to remain indefinitely a mere observer of these strange experiments and was ready for it when a doctor, at a meeting soon after, turned to me and said: "Now let us ask the American gentleman if he would care to volunteer...?"

I was thoroughly dubious but my curiosity was aroused and I agreed. I sat in a comfortable chair and was given the customary verbal suggestions that I was getting sleepy and relaxed and was going into a hypnotic trance. The doctor lifted my arm and suggested it was becoming heavy, relaxed and free from feeling. I was told my arm was just like a piece of wood, completely free from all feeling and incapable of experiencing pain.

I went along with all this and the doctor then told me that a sterilized hypodermic needle was to be plunged through the skin but I was assured I would feel nothing.

I watched in horror as he pinched the skin of my arm into a fold and drove the needle right through the two layers. I felt nothing during the insertion and removal of the needle.

The doctor then suggested that I should wake up feeling fresh and relaxed. I did precisely that. I woke up feeling fresh and relaxed, none the worse for the experience—but still uneasily skeptical. I was going to be a hard nut to crack.

I have had numerous inoculations in my lifetime without much distress so how was this different? Except that inoculations are usually simple jabs of a needle and do not penetrate two layers of skin with flesh in between.

To satisfy myself I challenged the doctor to repeat the exercise without first hypnotizing me. He obliged and the moment his needle pierced the skin I flinched away with a very real and undeniable sensation of pain. I was convinced—or at any rate convinced enough for one day.

Through this simple experience, however, I was convinced of the power of suggestion and the evidence showed pretty clearly, even to me, that the people with whom I was increasingly associating in this corner of the world had a knowledge—perhaps insight is a better word—of the secret workings of the mind which is not at all familiar to us in the West.

❊

My work took up most of my time. I did a good deal of travelling and also spent a lot of time on office work. There were reports to write, investigations to carry out, more reports to write. I did a fair amount of entertaining in the evenings and there was rarely much time left for anything else.

But never far from my thoughts were the youngster who mysteriously repeated the chalked words he hadn't seen, the holymen who watched with rapt interest, the practical doctors who prescribed the incredible in their surgeries instead of codeine.

In the bookshops I found plenty of literature and whenever I could I bought books on the subject. I read anything I could lay hands on which I thought might bring me a little nearer to understanding the strange phenomena I had seen.

And as I probed deeper into the subject I began seeking out religious scholars and teachers to hear just where Buddhism and meditation came into all this for there appeared to me to be some sort of parallel between the hypnosis we know and that ancient Eastern faith.

Nevertheless, the demands of my job prevented me from engaging in any further practical efforts to pursue the mystery until one day about a year after I had settled in Bangkok.

It was a particularly hot day and the oppressive atmosphere made office work irksome. I was irritable and decided the best thing to do was to get out for a breather. I remembered that a member of the psychical research group, Dr. Charoon, was spending three months as a monk in a local temple where most Thai Buddhists usually retreated after completing their professional studies. They devote the time to learning and practicing the doctrines of their faith.

I decided to drag him away from his studies and perhaps enjoy an hour or two's congenial company, with some not too serious conversation thrown in, and generally cool off in the peaceful environment of the temple. At the prospect I felt better already.

I found Dr. Charoon poring over his books at a huge wooden desk. He was alone and the place was mercifully cool. I was glad I'd come and began to explain that it had been impossible to stay cooped up in my office a moment longer on such a day while some others, without mentioning any names, could idle their time away in a temple. It is just possible that he could see I was not my usual self for his first words were "Relax, brother!"

"That's exactly why I'm here," I replied.

"Then this time you'll do it properly," he said. "You've obviously been having a trying day. You need to relax thoroughly, if only for a short time, then you'll feel refreshed and able to carry on."

It made sense, but I was not prepared for what followed.

"I shall hypnotize you and put you into a deep, relaxing sleep. When you wake up you will have forgotten all your office worries and be able to go back to work with renewed vigor."

I was not going to argue. I lay down on the floor on a straw mat and gazed up at the domed ceiling. Distantly I heard Dr. Charoon telling me I was relaxing, going to sleep, my limbs were getting heavy, I was going to sleep....

Then a strange thing happened. While I continued sleeping Dr. Charoon returned to his books and unknown to me a young naval officer, also in his monkhood, entered and sat down at the far end of the room to meditate, assuming the Buddhist lotus position with his legs crossed and his back rigid.

All appeared normal in this peaceful atmosphere and I was oblivious to everything while lying perfectly relaxed on my back. The calm of the situation was disturbed when Dr. Charoon glanced up from his reading and noticed my right arm slowly raising up in the air and then lowering.

He was quite startled for he knew I was in a deep hypnotic trance and he had never experienced such a manifestation before while a subject was under hypnosis. He walked excitedly over to where the naval officer was meditating, shook him and in amazement explained what he had just witnessed.

The naval officer grinned and said that while meditating he was mentally suggesting that I perform this action. He was testing his powers of mental telepathy.

Dr. Charoon was skeptical and challenged him to try again, this time with the mental suggestion that my left arm should be induced to rise and lower. Throughout this time I had no knowledge of anything unusual going on, I did not know the officer had come into the temple, I did not hear them talk and even if I had I would not have understood their language.

My left arm went up and down, then both arms, then my left leg followed by my right leg as well as various combinations of all my limbs according to the mental commands of the meditating naval officer.

The officer was vastly amused. Dr. Charoon was astonished. He brought me out of my hypnotic state and explained what had been happening. At first I could not understand what all the hilarity was about, or the excitement, but it struck all three of us that we had stumbled across some extraordinary evidence in support of ideas on the subject of extrasensory perception.

2

The Unknown Side of the Mind

My personal file in Washington is endorsed with the word "retired"—it is now, that is to say. Inside my personal file there's plenty of evidence that I'm not the type of man to be taken for a ride too easily.

I've knocked about the world on Government work since my teens visiting most countries and enjoying a rewarding and often exciting and strenuous life. I've had my share of scrapes. But on the whole I've carried out the business I had to do with success even when there were quite formidable obstacles.

I'm not, therefore, the kind of person to be fooled by a bunch of smiling holymen and medical crackpots in Thailand.

The more I got to know the Thais the more I liked them and the more I realized that the people I was mixing with were neither eccentrics nor poseurs. I was forced to the conclusion they were sincere and genuine seekers after truth. It was that simple, and yet to our Western ears the very phrase sounds naive.

That the Thais are a patient, easy-going race, never to be flustered, is undeniable. A typical scene at any railroad station is of a group of Thais sitting with their parcels on their laps and smiles on their faces waiting for the arrival of a train which could be an hour late.

Patience and endurance are inbred qualities, particularly among those born and raised in the Buddhist faith. Perhaps at the beginning of my assignment in Bangkok my Western friends tired of hearing me use the phrase "This wouldn't do back home." But I found I was saying and thinking it less and less. Perhaps after all, the philosophy by

11

which the Buddhist Thais lived could provide the key to the solution of some of the problems of our more sophisticated society.

Most of us know only too well we live at a pace which is too hectic. Some people find it impossible to keep up. Psychoanalysis must be one of the most profitable careers a youngster could go in for today.

We realize for example, that science and technology are now so advanced as to be practically beyond the understanding of any but the most specialized practitioners. Liver, kidney, heart, lung, brain and eye transplants are everyday occurrences. Computers work out our bank statements—usually correctly—and astronauts explore space with the aplomb of motorists heading for the coast on Sunday. Yet most of us understand nothing, and never will, of how these achievements are accomplished.

And worst of all, in the shadowy background we are uncomfortably aware that the science of warfare has developed to a point where a major confrontation, with everything unleashed, would be unthinkably disastrous.

So we don't think—or try not to. Instead we set our targets lower and aim to master what we call the art of living. We organize our lives and our jobs for maximum protection from the pressures that bear down on us from all sides. We work as hard as we need for pay checks that will provide the kind of cars, clothes, television sets and houses we think we should have. We organize holidays for summer, ski trips in winter, central heating, swimming pools. We even organize with great care the number of children it would be convenient to have in the family. We cushion ourselves in every way we can against a world which seems in danger of spinning too fast for us.

And if, in spite of all this meticulous planning, we begin to feel we're not coping very well with the art of living we hire the services of an analyst to sort out the priorities for us—we start examining the processes of our minds.

We are very different from the average Buddhist Thai. Not for us a long, patient wait at a station with the train well overdue and a smile creasing our good-humored faces. We expect the train to be on time; a few minutes late and we're checking our watches, anything longer and we're hounding the station master for an explanation. Usually there is an explanation. In Thailand there needn't be.

What then, does a Buddhist Thai have that a Westerner has not? I decided to find out, to investigate the whole subject in depth so far as my work allowed time for the necessary research.

At this point an interruption occurred which could have brought to an abrupt end my proposed inquiries, but instead, redirected them into a related channel. I was recalled to Washington for a three-month briefing at headquarters. I packed my bags, said my goodbyes and left Bangkok promising my friends I'd be back soon.

On the plane I had time to reflect. My strange experience at the temple pointed to certain obvious conclusions. The naval officer had "suggested" my actions during his meditation and aimed his somewhat playful thoughts towards me while I was in an hypnotic state—not wholly insensible as in ordinary sleep but physically asleep, mentally relaxed, yet sufficiently aware to receive and act on another's suggestions apparently passed by thought transference or telepathy.

When the situation had been explained to me and after I had recovered from the initial astonishment—and skepticism—we tried in vain to repeat the entire incident.

I was hypnotized, the naval man resumed his meditation and his attempts at thought transference and—nothing happened. If it really happened the first time failure the second time could only be caused by one factor: we were trying too hard.

It was obvious. We were determined to see the astonishing experiments repeated because our curiosity had been aroused. Of course it wouldn't work. In the original circumstances the incident was spontaneous; this time nobody was relaxed. How could we be?

In fact we were all hard at work. With whatever mental faculties remained conscious under my hypnotic state, which must have been only partial, I was hard at it trying to receive signals that never came. The navy man was desperately pushing out unspoken instructions that never even penetrated his bald cranium. The element of complete detachment was gone and if our repeated attempts to recapture it were never again successful at least we thought we knew why.

In Washington I reported for duty, revived old friendships, dated one or two of the more attractive typists at headquarters and generally reoriented myself in preparation for the temporary change of scene. I was suddenly back in the West, with its familiar smells, familiar noises and familiar people.

After only a day or two, however, I received a message—by letter, not thought transference—from a member of that group of amiable psychics in Bangkok, a dentist named Dr. Prapan. He was at the University of Alabama taking a course on medical hypnotism and wrote that if I had time he would like to see me.

Somehow Dr. Prapan had come to hear of the temple incident and he felt we might both learn something of interest from a visit to Duke University, in North Carolina, where Professor J. B. Rhine had been running a parapsychology laboratory and conducting investigations into extrasensory and psychic phenomena since the early 1930s.

The idea intrigued me. After a week or two I fixed myself a few days' leave and motored south through the apple orchards and cotton plantations of Virginia to keep my appointment. Dr. Prapan, away from his home environment, was just as I remembered him and he grinned as we shook hands. A short fellow with a high-pitched voice, a little timid, very courteous, he seemed to be enjoying his stay in the U.S. and had only one reservation to make about the cordial hospitality he'd received in the Deep South. He had found the color segregation in those parts embarrassing—in an ironical way.

The first time he traveled on a bus he saw the Colored passengers occupying the segregated rear seats and, afraid he might enrage the Whites by presuming to sit with them, he chose a seat at the back.

"But I was spotted by someone at the front," he said, "and he shouted at me in a loud voice, 'Hey you, you're not a Nigger, you sit up here' and he dragged me up to the front of the bus to sit with the Whites."

I could sympathize with the poor Dr. Prapan in his embarrassment. The conduct of the well-meaning American was no doubt acutely painful to the Thai's sensibilities.

Eventually we set off for Durham and Duke University where we had arranged for an interview with the Professor. Duke is a university on the grand scale with impressive architecture, ivy covered stone walls and I believe one of the largest campuses in the States. The parapsychology lab was a separate building standing on its own and we introduced ourselves to the receptionist at the door. She had evidently been warned to expect us and immediately led the way to

Professor Rhine's office. We couldn't help being impressed with the size and spaciousness of the place.

The Professor greeted us politely and after we had told him of our interest in extrasensory phenomena following the affair in the Thai temple and the experiments we had seen he went to great lengths to explain to us the work and objectives of the laboratory. Then he took us on a tour of the lab.

We met several of the students and watched them at work with a variety of curious apparatus. In some cases they were being helped in experiments by volunteers who acted as guinea pigs for tests of extrasensory and clairvoyant ability. Dr. J. G. Pratt, statistician, mathematician and student of the science of chance, who has worked with Rhine since the early pioneering days, described experiments he had carried out to demonstrate that the mind could exercise control over material objects.

The equipment of the lab consisted of gaming tables, mechanical dice throwers, machinery for automatic card shuffling and the like. Some of the students we spoke to were engaged in analyzing statements made by persons who had experienced strange examples of extrasensory perception, premonition, dreams and thoughts which turned out to be prophetic of future events.

In one recorded case, for instance, a mother whose son had gone to sea was wakened in the night by an extreme sensation of being choked with water. She had been in a thoroughly shocked state and it took an hour for her husband to persuade her to return to bed and try to get back to sleep. Later, it turned out her boy was drowned in an accident at almost exactly the time she had her nightmare. Scientists at the Rhine lab had investigated the affair in minute detail in an effort to find the mental link which had communicated the boy's horror to his mother hundreds of miles away.

Scores of similar happenings were recorded in the Duke archives and work had been carried out to detect by what so far undiscovered mental processes such events could occur. Among them were many instances in the 1939-1945 war in which mothers, sisters or sweethearts had experienced a *feeling* that their sons, brothers or boy friends had been injured or killed at the battle fronts which later turned out to be true. They had recorded many cases in which relatives had had an uncanny yet quite certain feeling that their aunts or cousins had died in the London Blitz, only to be informed days afterwards that these tragedies had indeed taken place.

Professor Rhine, elderly, scholarly, with white hair brushed straight back, was immersed in his subject. A pioneer of intensive experimental work on telepathy and clairvoyance, he told us he preferred the term "parapsychology" to "psychical research" because of the implication of the occult and spiritual associations of "psychical" and he preferred the term "extrasensory perception" to "thought transference," "clairvoyance," and "telepathy." Strange manifestations of the subconscious—we've all at some time or another visited a place for the first time and had the spooky feeling we know what we'll see around the next corner or who we're going to meet next— these are his science.

With infinite care and patience, and always with the frustrating knowledge that their researches frequently lead to a dead end of inconclusiveness, he and his team were piecing together the scraps of data which might one day spark off a glimmer of light and point the way to some eagerly sought answers.

A number of absorbing and readable books have resulted from their labors, among them *The Reach Of The Mind* in which Rhine relates the development of Duke University as a major contributor to present-day knowledge of this mysterious and neglected subject.

So far during my visit to Duke I had, however, learned nothing which added positively to my understanding. Dr. Prapan and I had, to be sure, seen the most unusual laboratory of all time and listened to some very strange stories but it all seemed to be getting us no further than square one.

As we were getting ready to leave Professor Rhine reached into his desk drawer and produced a pack of cards. They looked the same as ordinary playing cards from the back, but on the face side, instead of the familiar patterns of hearts, diamonds, clubs and spades each card carried a symbol, a circle, a star, a wavy line, a cross or a square. There were twenty-five cards in all, five of each symbol.

"Have a look at these E.S.P. cards," he said. "We've used them a great deal at Duke. Now if you're really interested in clairvoyance or telepathy here's a simple test you can try out on each other."

Dr. Prapan and I looked at each other.

The Professor shuffled the deck and placed it face down on the table. "Take one, look at it and don't show me," he said. "I'll guess which symbol you're looking at—and the chances are I'll be wrong. Try it."

I picked up the first card. It was a star. Professor Rhine looking deep into my eyes, said it was a circle. I took up a circle, he said it was a wavy line. We continued for three or four more cards and then gave it up. Rhine was right twice. I was puzzled.

"So what does that prove?" I asked.

"It proves that I do not guess at all accurately and that my clairvoyant ability leaves much to be desired."

He smiled and I waited for him to go on.

"This test, and variants of it, have been done many thousands of times," he said. "The average number of correct guesses is five out of twenty-five. As the number of correct guesses grows so do the odds against chance playing a part in it grow also. The element of clairvoyance or extrasensory perception comes into play.

"If chance was the only factor which decided the number of correct guesses it would be impossible to guess right twenty-five times out of the twenty-five. Not impossible," he corrected himself, "but the odds against such a result would be astronomically high, into millions. So high they amount to impossibility."

Nevertheless, high scores had been achieved. He told me of an experiment which he and Dr. Pratt carried out with a subject named Pearce. Pratt was in a building a hundred yards away with Rhine while Pearce remained in the laboratory building. The E.S.P. cards were used in fifteen experimental sessions in conditions of utmost security and there were 750 guesses in all. Pearce averaged nine correct out of twenty-five over the entire run, four more than the expectation of chance, a remarkably high score and valuable evidence of the subject's clairvoyant abilities. The odds against such a high score were, said Rhine, a hundred million million million to one. No subject tested at Duke since then had matched it.

There had been criticism of the tests done at Duke, said Rhine. Not on matters of authenticity, for the strictest precautions were maintained which no scientist could reasonably challenge, but on the question of the value of the work. Although many eminent scientists both in the States and in Britain and Europe had conducted similar work and were watching the Duke results with growing interest, science as a whole remained skeptical and tended to dismiss the study of E.S.P. as an unworthy or unproductive line of research.

"In spite of the amount of evidence that the subconscious has some kind of measurable influence it has not so far been taken up as a subject which deserves proper scientific study," he said. There was of course a growing awareness that the mind could produce physical effects upon the body, causing illnesses that could only be cured by psychologically treating the mind, but in the broader application science as a whole was inclined to evade the issue.

"Clairvoyance, prophesy and precognition have been established facts for centuries," he added, "particularly in countries where the people's culture has been dominated by religion."

We rose to go, but I told the Professor I was still a little in the dark on the E.S.P. cards. He seemed to be spelling out in words of one syllable what was plainly obvious: that it was unlikely that anyone could guess the symbols on the cards right every time.

"Keep the cards and try the test on each other, remembering that when chance alone is involved you are not likely to get more than five right out of twenty-five. Anything over that and you are bringing your clairvoyant ability or E.S.P. into play. And it would be interesting," he said as a parting shot, "to take note of the circumstances in which the highest scores are obtained."

Dr. Prapan and I drove away from Duke with a good deal to think about. I was particularly anxious to discover some relevance between the E.S.P. card trick and the genuine experiences of thought transference which had been observed in Bangkok. It was not until some time later that I was able to draw significant conclusions on the connection.

We motored to Washington and every stop we made at restaurants and motels on the way was a chance to call the cards. It was an entertaining pastime. We generally made scores of five or less but one time I guessed seven correct which pleased us both. According to the Rhine findings my achievement was higher than chance alone would account for.

Back at headquarters I tried the test on several of my friends and office colleagues. Always I came up with the same result: the average stayed around four to six.

Then I remembered Allen, and with Allen came the big breakthrough. He had an apartment in the same building as mine and I knew before I approached him that he'd want to have nothing to do with the cards.

Allen was an extrovert type. He moved in the big-time sailing set in the South Pacific, had his own catamaran. He was creative, intellectually bright and had little patience with my sudden interest in extrasensory perception and things of the mind.

Nevertheless, I was determined to pin him down to at least one session at cards.

Predictably, he didn't want to know. Would I please take a walk or find something to do? He was busy. I knew Allen was busy. He had recently resigned from Government service and was planning to set up in business on his own account. As an expert electrical engineer he was held in great esteem and it was his intention to start a firm to install and service electronic equipment on commercial and private aircraft.

His place was littered with catalogues and price quotations of the equipment he planned to buy for his new company. He was totally absorbed in plans for the future. A guessing game with a deck of cards had no place in his plans. I had to prod him for a week before he gave way under the pressure. He made one condition, however. That after one test I would undertake not to bother him again. I agreed.

I shuffled the cards and told him I was ready to proceed. He was making a calculation but obligingly looked up for a moment.

"Star," he said. I marked a tick but said nothing. There was a long pause while he sorted through some papers. I held up the next card and he adjusted his glasses.

"A star again," he said. He was right and I put a tick and said nothing. He lit a cigarette and went to a bookcase to search for a leaflet that turned out to be on the table in front of him. He cursed gently and thumbed through the pages for a diagram he thought he'd seen. I held up another card.

"You still here?" he said. I said I was. "That's…a diamond." He was cooperating, but the cards were receiving the least of his attention. He was out West working on his new laboratory. The plant necessary for some possible future order was the only consideration of any importance at the moment. He lit another cigarette.

It took almost an hour to wade through the twenty-five cards.

He scored the extraordinary total of twenty-three correct guesses.

I tried to explain to Allen how exceptional his performance was and at first he showed no more interest than before. Later, however, he put aside his catalogue having worked enough for one evening and began to listen. I told him about the tests conducted at the Rhine laboratory and that a score anything over seven was considered remarkable.

This must have appealed to his vanity for he suggested we go through the test again—to confirm that he was an unusual subject. This was quite an about-turn for Allen so we tried again.

"Star," he called. Wrong.

"Wavy line," wrong again. We went through the cards again and again that night and on successive evenings that week. He raised scores of three, four and never more than five each time.

Allen lost interest, not unnaturally. For me the experiments proved to be a turning point. A very high score had been obtained when Allen's mental concentration had been directed elsewhere: peanuts when he had given his full attention to the tests.

When I got back to my office in Bangkok I turned my attention to the influence which religion had on the minds of my Thai associates. Unaccountable manifestations of little known areas of mental activity like clairvoyance and E.S.P. were a line of study which were an attractive novelty with an undeniable relevance to my search. I am convinced that it's only a matter of time before a significant breakthrough will occur, to the surprise of all concerned.

But they did not occupy a great proportion of the attention which Easterners gave to the actions of the mind in daily life. On that score the religious traditions of the past were of infinitely greater importance.

3

The Prince Who Searched for "Truth"

A LONG time ago a young man sat down under a tree in Northern India and resolved not to move until he understood the realities of life. It was some task.

I felt a bit like that as I flew back to Thailand from Washington. Was there an actual cause for every effect? A stone falls if you push it, but what is the cause, for example, of a premonition which turns out to be correct or a dream which accurately foretells a future happening? There are too many recorded examples of this to be brushed aside as of no consequence. Shakespeare put the mystery in a sentence when he gave one of his characters the remark "There are more things in heaven and earth, Horatio, than are dreamed on in our philosophy."

The young man's circumstances and background were very different from mine, however, and his uneasy thoughts about life and its meaning had certainly been preying on his mind far longer than mine had.

His name was Gotama. He was a prince. His father ruled the kingdom of Kapilavatthu near the borders of Nepal. The date: twenty-five centuries ago. From accounts that have come down to us we receive the impression that the youth, though a loved and loving son, gave his royal parents a worrying time. He spent many hours immersed in his thoughts and cared little for the responsibilities of a future ruler. He was preoccupied with the spiritual aspects of suffering and mixed with yogis and holymen probably too much for his father's liking.

The king decided to bring the boy to his senses once and for all by marrying him off at the age of 18 to the beautiful princess Yasodhara. The plan worked—for a time. The king became a grandfather and Gotama and Yasodhara stayed together happily for twelve years.

But although Gotama bore all the outward signs of a respectable, if somewhat withdrawn, scion of the royal family his heart was not completely in the job. Never far from the surface, so the legends go, was the yearning for knowledge, the questing for "truth," the itch to know the reasons why and the answers to the unanswerable questions about life and death, living and suffering.

Like everyone else of his day he believed that life was unending—when a soul reached the end of its present existence it moved on into another. He did not question the ancient Brahmanic doctrine of the cycle of lives. But if one continued to live, albeit in other bodies, was it necessary also to suffer? What was the meaning, and the purpose, of pain?

It was probably because he was a prince, and with the thought that he would one day be the head of a nation and therefore responsible to a large extent for his people's welfare, that he decided to find out—or at least satisfy himself that he had tried.

He shaved his head and his beard, put away his regal ornaments and rich garments, clothed himself in the rough yellow habit of a religious mendicant and left his luxurious palace/prison on foot.

There are many accounts of how the young Prince Gotama spent the next six years and at this distance in time the details are blurred. It is known he studied the teachings of the Brahmans but found they did not provide the answers to the mysteries he yearned to solve.

He moved for a time among a group of ascetics who practiced self-inflicted flesh mortifying torture in the hope of gaining peace. He found this was useless and led nowhere. He came under the spell of two great yogis who had attained high degrees of supernormal psychical powers and for a time he read their teachings and practiced their beliefs.

Still he was not satisfied that this line of thought, pursued in conditions of rigorous asceticism, fasting and self-denial, which must have severely affected his health, led to the path of peace. Peace of mind, the solutions to the mind's question marks, the meaning of life; all evaded the young prince.

Six years elapsed; then it dawned on Gotama, by now thin and exhausted and perhaps looking a good deal older than his thirty or so years, that his search was in fact achieving one important result. By process of elimination he was arriving at some kind of truth even if it was only negative. He was discovering where true peace and understanding did not reside and this in itself was a revelation that gave him hope.

What we call "transcendental" meditation was widely practiced (it may even have been induced by drugs contained in certain common foods) and, resolving to abandon his ardent and exhausting searching day after day, year after year, Gotama settled instead on the "Middle Way." With a new calmness he began to look into the true nature of life. Sitting under a bodhi tree he plunged into profound meditation which lasted several weeks and emerged at last into a state of enlightenment in which he understood the cause of suffering and consequently its cure.

The young prince, devoted to his wife and family but whose longing for the true meanings of life had thrown him from the happiness and warmth of a rich life into the wilderness of doubt and suffering, now achieved his ultimate joy. He arose from the shade of the bodhi tree, stretched the numbness from his limbs and began the long trek home to the arms of his loved ones.

Wherever he went he spread the news of what he had learned, what he had at last understood. His mind was clear: there were no more questions. And he found he was able to impart his newfound understanding to others.

His wife was one of his first converts but he traveled widely through Northern India and his fame went before him, the crowds flocked to see the "Awakened One," the "Enlightened One," and hear him expound his gospel. His words were repeated again and again long after he had moved on.

Today about one third of humanity follow the teachings of Gotama the Buddha and find in its refreshingly simple formula an effective antidote to the harsh realities of life.

❀

I have pieced together in very abbreviated form the story of the foundation of Buddhism as it was retold to me by various Thai friends, but it is certain that the full facts surrounding the emergence of the religion so long ago can be no more accurate than those surrounding the life of Christ.

Like Christ, Gotama the Buddha was a teacher. He spoke to groups of men who stopped him on his way and gave spiritual help where it was sought. He was a compulsive preacher who practiced what he preached. But his communication was by word of mouth; he did not pause to write it down and there were no newspaper reporters in those days to catch his phrases and record them for future generations. It is amusing to compare the situation of Buddha with that of a modem evangelist who has the benefit of the Press and television to spread his gospel and create interest among a mass audience. Buddha had no such advantages. Word of mouth was his only medium yet his message spread rapidly throughout Northern India and, eventually, to neighboring continents and throughout the rest of the known world.

Thus, then, was the beginning of Buddhism. Now, as I sped by a jet towards Bangkok and reunion with my mysterious Oriental friends, I reflected on Buddha's thoughts and the kind of simple logic by which a Buddhist follower is supposed to reach a state of bliss.

From the start I knew I was at a disadvantage. There is something in the Thai character, as I have said, which is strangely missing from mine. It has something to do with the ability to stay quiet, to sit still, to be impassive, long-suffering, patient. Like other Westerners I am an intellectual animal and have an irrepressible urge to use my mind on a positive thinking level.

There are bodhi trees in Thailand today and I have often admired their gracefulness—they are high, shaped like an upturned wineglass and have large heart shaped leaves—but I could no more sit in the shade of a bodhi tree and meditate upon the truth about life for weeks without stirring, than sit through a movie, however brilliantly filmed and acted, twice in one afternoon. It just is not me.

The subject had me under its spell and I read a great deal and exchanged views in conversation with others but when the act of meditation was mentioned it was, for me, just part of the general scene, an area to be taken into account but a far, far too tedious and boring undertaking actually to try out for myself.

After all, I seldom sat still for more than a few minutes at a time so how could I be expected to assume the uncomfortable lotus position and keep it for long enough to make the experience worth while? My mind was active: how could I bring it to a standstill, clear it of its commonplace encumbrances—and would this produce the right results anyway?

When the plane dropped down over the airfield at Bangkok I had the feeling that some of the answers might be within reach if I looked in the right places.

4

A Religion or a Way of Life?

WESTERNERS generally regard Buddhism not as a religion but as a philosophy of life. Essentially this is true. The young prince Gotama, through his vision and penetrating wisdom, became revered as Buddha, "The Awakened One," but it was his teaching that captured the imagination of the masses.

Buddha came to understand that the destiny of beings was not a result of mere chance or fate, nor was it dependent upon the arbitrary actions of a supreme being. Man's destiny could be traced to former deeds, good and bad.

He devised the Law of Dependent Origination of all phenomena—the law of cause and effect. He found that for every action there is an equal and opposite reaction.

Thus he explained the sufferings of the sick and the unhappy as retribution and directly traceable to misdeeds done in former lives—the moral law of cause and effect.

According to Buddhist philosophy every deed—mental, oral or physical—has a consequence. The entire universe is governed by moral principles. Any attempt to act contrary to these principles or disregard them will only result in the increase of suffering.

Wise and wholesome deeds performed under moral principles reduce suffering and bring happiness, while unwise and unwholesome actions carried out without regard to moral principles result in the end in the increase of woe and suffering.

Since karma, the impetus for action, comes from the mind which is continually evolving and changing, the effects of the karma are also continually changing, constituting the various vicissitudes of all lives.

Let me try to explain.

The goal of all Buddhists is the attainment of *nirvana,* a state in which ignorance and desires are dispelled and suffering ceases. The *Dhamma,* the name given to the universal moral law discovered by Buddha, will lead the devout Buddhist to this state.

It is summed up in the Four Noble Truths: universal suffering, the origin of suffering, its extinction and the path leading to its extinction.

The First Noble Truth concerning the "Universality of Suffering" teaches that all forms of existence are subject to suffering.

Life is in reality a disease and is always accompanied by three inevitable characteristics, *anicca, dukkha* and *anattā.*

Anicca means change, impermanence or transitoriness.

Dukkha means suffering, unendurability, unsatisfactoriness, sorrowfulness.

Anattā means egolessness, not self, insubstantiality, impersonality of existence.

The Second Noble Truth is about the "Origin of Suffering" and teaches that the cause of suffering is ignorance and desire—and with cause, effect will surely follow. "That nothing can come to be except that it be dependent on preceding causes and present supporting conditions."

Everything that has arisen, without exception, has done so in dependence upon some immediately preexisting condition, and that with the abrogation of this condition the thing arising in dependence upon it is also abrogated.

The Third Noble Truth is concerned with the "Ending of Suffering." It shows how, through the extinction of desire and ignorance, suffering will cease and freedom be attained.

Since desire, the thirst for life or death, is the origin and cause of suffering, when the cause ceases, the effect (the suffering) also ceases.

The Fourth Noble Truth shows the way this goal comes to the follower of Buddhism. It is "The Eightfold Path" of Right Understanding, Right Resolution, Right Speech, Right Bodily Deeds, Right Livelihood, Right Effort, Right Mindfulness and Right Concentration of Mind.

These moral laws as expounded by Buddha are common to most religions. The difference from other religions is this. One cannot fully accept the teaching without actively participating in actions which lead one to experience these truths for oneself. Blind acceptance of another's opinion is of no use.

Thus the truth becomes a fact instead of a theory for the person following the Buddha's teachings.

Right Understanding

To understand the Buddhist code fully requires a great deal of practical study and also exercises in practical meditation.

Too much intellectual speculation, which can be valueless and a waste of time, may lead to a blind alley.

By practical living of the teachings of Buddha and through intuitive insight gained through meditation one can have Right Understanding.

Right Resolution

This is the firm resolution to live according to the laws of reality and to persevere until freedom is attained. The resolution is not to be applied to the attainment of any pleasures but to attain a perfect attitude of mind.

Right Speech

This means not to lie, slander, or speak harshly to bring harm to fellow beings; to use wise words for the comfort and edification of others.

Right Bodily Deeds

This means to refrain from intentional killing or harming of any living creature, abstaining from stealing and sexual misconduct.

Right Livelihood

This means not to have any occupation or profession which brings harm or suffering to others.

Right Effort

This is perseverance in the overcoming of old, and avoiding new, bad actions by speech, body and mind; and the effort to maintain old, and develop new, actions of righteousness, inner peace and wisdom.

RIGHT MINDFULNESS

This is alertness of mind, an ever ready mental clearness in whatever we are doing, speaking or thinking, and keeping before our mind the realities of existence, namely the impermanence, unsatisfactoriness and impersonal nature of all forms of existence.

To be silently aware of the true nature of the moment without interpretation. To be continually impersonally aware of the true nature of perceptions, body movements, thoughts and objects, entirely free from worldly greed and grief.

RIGHT CONCENTRATION OF MIND

This is concentration directed towards morally wholesome objects with the purpose of obliterating the mental hindrances of sensual lust, ill will, mental stiffness and dullness, restlessness and anxiety, and wavering doubt or skepticism.

Such mental discipline induces a tranquillity which forms a strong foundation for the development of wisdom. Concentrate on the inner working of oneself and one gains penetrating insight into the real nature of existence.

It is simply the practical study of self, or of that which gives the illusion of self, and thereby coming to the transcendence of self.

Right Concentration consists of two steps—*samādhi* and *vipassanā*. Samādhi leads to perfect tranquillity while vipassanā leads to true knowledge and wisdom.

Samādhi consists of concentration of mind on morally wholesome objects and is used to quiet the usual frantic jumping around of numerous thoughts.

❋

There are various methods in use throughout the East by which this concentration is attained, such as the repetition of a word or phrase or of a wholesome thought as practiced by some famous Indian teachers, or the observing of the rising and falling movement of the navel while breathing. Concentration on the touch of the air as it enters the nose while breathing, or the observation of a pinpoint of light or other wholesome material objects can be used.

When the Beatles were introduced to meditation in India to the accompaniment of much excitement and publicity their teacher, the

30

Maharishi Mahesh Yogi, advised them to pick any word that appealed to them and repeat it over and over to themselves in silence. It was one method of inducing concentration.

Samādhi, when properly performed, gives a feeling of rest and relaxation. When the concentration is intense the mind goes into mental states beyond the fivefold senses' activity and is attainable only in solitude and by unremitting perseverance in the practice of concentration.

Although the outer sense impressions have ceased, the mind remains active, perfectly alert, fully awake.

As the mind goes deeper into concentration it is filled with rapture and happiness born of solitude and detachment. The normal thinking processes are left behind, there is a state of simple existence, full relaxation and tranquillity.

As concentration deepens, delight and pleasure are transcended without any anticipation of happiness to come. Still deeper, the ideas of pleasure and pain, good and evil, joy and sorrow, are transcended. There are no traces of feeling, there is a state of one-pointedness of mind and complete and utter equanimity.

It is at this stage that the mind is perfectly purified, perfectly translucent, free from flaw, tranquil and may be bent according to Buddhist philosophy towards the attainment of supernormal powers or towards the absolute permanent clearing of all evils and impurities from the mind.

Vipassanā consists of contemplation on the phenomena that are actually happening in oneself and one's body. One gains through clear experience an insight into the true nature of all bodily and mental phenomena being characterized by impermanence, unsatisfactoriness, and impersonality.

In vipassanā the mind is bent towards the full knowledge of the inner working and true nature of the supposed self.

One reaches the point of enlightenment at which ignorance of the true nature of existence and all forms of craving are destroyed and completely cleansed away, even into the deepest region of the unconscious mind.

The illusion of self is now fully understood and transcended, the Four Noble Truths realized and nirvana attained. Reality is thus proved and verified through one's own realization and experience.

A subtle combination of samādhi and vipassanā brings about an early understanding, for samādhi enhances the development of vipassanā and vipassanā enhances the development of samādhi.

These, then, are the laws and the philosophy of Buddhism. To a novice like me it all sounded rather complicated and awesome but obviously very, very good if the facts were as the theory promised.

When I had settled into my routine once again I decided to look into the practical side of meditation.

I located a temple in Bangkok offering courses in meditation and made inquiries about the possibilities of enrolling. I was to be surprised by the reception they gave me.

5

Beautiful Temple, Harrowing Experience

I PURPOSELY didn't reveal to colleagues at the office the extent of my growing interest in Buddhism and the science of the mind because I feared an unsympathetic response. And when, having assimilated as much theory as I could cope with for the time being, I decided to investigate the practical side of meditation, I left my friends to guess how I intended to spend my next two-weeks' leave. By conventional Western standards my conduct was becoming positively eccentric.

The Thais told me that courses in meditation were offered at several temples in Bangkok and so, not without some misgivings, I made up my mind to take the plunge. The beautiful Wat Mahatai was the temple I chose—a wonderful and ornate complex of buildings near the Thamasat University and in the area of the Royal Palace, the setting of that great love story which became the hit musical *The King and I.*

Today the palace, which for hundreds of years was at the hub of this strange country's culture, is merely one of Thailand's tourist attractions—and I felt a little like a tourist myself as I approached the great doors of the temple nearby. A little nervous, and feeling distinctly out of my element, I passed through the main entrance and told a saffron robed monk standing just inside that I had an appointment with the abbot.

Evidently I was expected for the man hurried away and returned almost immediately with the head monk, who was also the chief instructor, and a young student in casual Western clothes with an open necked sports shirt. In Thailand, students frequently use the temples as places to live and study, much as Western students often seek the quiet of a public library.

The student—all smiles and courtesy in the usual Thai manner—was Somboon. Somboon was to be my interpreter and an excellent job he made of it: without him I would have achieved scant progress for I had not at this time mastered the difficult language. The sound of the Thai tongue is hard enough to follow but written manuscript is worse: it is read from left to right—but without any space between the words.

The authorities at the temple were plainly delighted to have me as a serious student. The fact of a foreigner showing an interest in their religion, and the prospects of assisting a stranger along the path of practical insight, gave them a good deal of pleasure and they made quite a fuss of me. They seemed to smile even more than usual, but I soon realized the members of the temple community, with their natural good humour, had something out of the ordinary to smile about. The average Thai comes to about five feet five inches in height; the chief instructor happened also to be about the same across the middle, and he was escorting round the temple a bulky United States citizen who towered over everyone's head to a height of six foot two.

In the austere confines of the temple this unusual spectacle gave rise to some discreet mirth until the inmates grew accustomed to having me among them.

"I will introduce you to all the instructors first," said the abbot by way of the young Somboon. "Then we'll get down to work."

When these formalities were over and I had paid my respects in the customary Thai manner he led me into a large hall. It was to be my home, bedroom, dining room and meditation chamber. About the size of a basketball court, the room contained no furniture except a small altar and a few mats scattered over the wooden floor. I began to feel there might, after all, be more congenial ways of spending two-weeks' leave, but the portly instructor had a look of calm and tranquillity that inspired confidence and I vowed to keep my spirits up for what I hoped would be a most rewarding and peaceful experience.

"I wish you to read these pamphlets," said the instructor benignly, "and secondly I must have your promise that you will pay strict obedience to me and follow all my instructions and guidance."

I told him he had my word and that I intended to be a model student if it was in my power. I had read a great deal of the theory and was impressed with what I had both read and heard; now I meant to take my researches a stage further by trying it out for myself.

Wat Mahatai, Bangkok, Thailand

He seemed satisfied and went away, leaving me to ponder my situation and peruse the leaflets he had given me. They explained the course of instruction in simple terms and, luckily, English.

When the instructor returned he stayed with me for only a short time. The first lesson was simple and dealt with the fundamentals.

"It would be best to take the lotus posture," he began. "It is the best position for training exercises. Do as I do."

He selected a floor mat and sat down with, I thought, surprising lightness and agility for a man of his globular dimensions. He held his back straight and crossed his legs in front of him. With his shaven head and eyebrows, his general roundness and tranquil, smiling face I could not help thinking how much he resembled one of those marble Chinese icons of Buddha himself.

I followed his movements, slumping heavily to the floor and crossing my knees as he had done.

"You may feel a little uncomfortable at first but this will soon pass," he said reassuringly. I was in agony already. A jarred nerve shot a line of pain along my left thigh.

There was a long pause as we both got used to the situation. I tried to return his serene smile.

"Look at your belly," he said suddenly. I glanced down anxiously. "You will try to keep the mind on the abdomen and come to know the movement of rising and falling." He paused again while I did this.

"Make a mental note of "rising" for the upward movement … and "falling" for the downward movement. If any difficulty is experienced you will place both hands on the abdomen…so to reinforce the impression."

We both did this for a minute or two.

"Contemplation on this body movement is used because it is continuous and automatic. It gives the mind something to latch on to in the initial stages of quieting the mind. Now carry on with this and I will see you again this evening."

The instructor rose lightly to his feet in a single motion and left the chamber. I was alone.

I gazed down at my belly, then at my knees. They were white where the bones pressed against the flesh in their unfamiliar, cramped position. I placed my hands on the flesh of my stomach and self-consciously fingered an obtrusive roll of fat which my desk job with the Government had encouraged.

I felt the rising and falling, rising and falling…and fell to musing on thoughts of lofty magnitude. Outside the sky was bright, framed by the temple windows into rectangles of purest blue. My back sagged and I straightened it with a jerk. Upwards, downwards. Upwards, downwards. I must meditate, I thought. Relax.

I noticed the persistent tick of my wristwatch. Tick, tick, tick, tick. Time must be getting on, I thought. But time didn't signify. There was no hurry. Out of habit I looked at the dial of my watch. Ten-thirty. Ten-thirty! How would I get through the day?

I had told Lulu, my maid, to bring me something nice in the way of cold lunch at around 11:30 a.m., which was the time when the inhabitants of the temple had their last meal of the day. I was feeling hungry already, but managed to convince myself it was sheer habit. I was here to meditate, contemplate my abdomen, and this I was going to do. Eating would follow later if necessary.

I looked down again and tried genuinely to clear my mind. Upward and downward, upward and downward. Rising, falling ....

Somewhere about this stage I must have nodded off for I was suddenly aware of someone beside me, the rustle of paper wrappers and the sound of a cup being placed on the floor at my side. It was Lulu. I denied being asleep and murmured thanks. Lunch was served. I made a move to get up on my feet and felt a sharp sensation of tightness and pain in my knee joints. Inch by inch I rose and stretched the stiffness out of my limbs. As the use came back into my body I stamped my feet on the floor, flung my arms sideways and upwards and felt the circulation begin to flow again.

When I had walked round the room three or four times I settled down, so to speak, to a stand-up meal and gave thanks for the faithful Lulu who had come to the rescue of a boss who was rapidly coming to regard himself as some kind of a crank.

But when, refreshed and nourished by the simple meal, I returned to the lotus posture sitting on the floor and resumed my exercises I found the whole idea was taking effect. The position was uncomfortable and disconcerting. I felt my joints would break open. But in time I found I could clear my mind of external things and focus it inwards.

I found it *did* help to gaze on the unlovely curves of my gently heaving belly and think of nothing more complicated than the upward, downward, rising, falling movements. If there was a way which led to a quiet mind, flushed out, uncluttered, this could be it.

Shortly after dusk Somboon reappeared and led me to the instructor for a debriefing on the day's activities. I spent most of the time complaining about the discomfort of the entire procedure.

"All is well, all is going fine," he said. "I am pleased at the progress you have made."

I was given instructions for the next day's exercises and these turned out to be an extension of what had gone before.

The author and his first meditation teacher

"You must now give attention to the rising and falling of all mental activities," said the sage.

"Thoughts, intentions, ideas, imaginings—all these mental happenings are not to be disregarded but must be followed up as soon as they occur.

"Make a mental note at the time of occurrence of all such activities. Thinking, reflecting, understanding, wandering, going, reaching, meeting, speaking, intending, bending, straightening—think of all these as they occur and consider each of them. Nothing must pass unnoticed through your mind."

Two days later I was ready to be carried away in a straitjacket, but the instructor praised me for the excellent progress I was making. On the fourth day my instructions became, if anything, even more rigorous. I was ordered to maintain the lotus posture and carry on with contemplation—with this subtle variation that I must stay perfectly still for a period of not less than an hour. No movement from the set position would be allowed.

"You will experience an intense feeling of tiredness and stiffness in the body and limbs," I was warned. "When such is the case keep your mind on the place where this feeling occurs and contemplate the thought "tired," "stiff," "painful," or whatever sensation you feel.

"But if pain becomes unbearable and you have to change position you must note "intending" and "changing" as before. You will make mental notes of all body sensations and movements."

Most of the next few days were spent in contemplating every single action, thought and movement. I was beginning to get the picture and the picture was making some sense. The mind in these strange circumstances does not focus on new life features, just unfamiliar ones. It turns in upon itself and examines the simple, everyday events of the self which are so commonplace that they become uncommon as subjects of our attention.

I soldiered on, my thoughts concentrated inward. I contemplated standing, sitting, seeing, looking, walking, lifting, putting up and down, stopping, stretching, touching, bringing, hot and cold, rising, falling, reaching, lying, spitting, sleeping, being drowsy, waking up, preparing, straightening, shutting, chewing, swallowing, hearing, smelling, being lazy, doubtful, tired, sorry, happy, blissful.

I even contemplated thinking itself. But the sensation that kept on recurring, and about which I found myself thinking more than others, was that of pain. By this time I was in intense and practically continuous agony. I was aching from head to foot. Even my hair ached.

In the end this searing discomfort, together with unutterable boredom, drove me to finish my session at the temple of Wat Mahatai ahead of schedule. Another day and I felt I would go crazy. I sought out my instructor and told Somboon to explain to him that I was through. I was sorry but I just could not finish the course—valuable and enlightening though it was.

"You have done well, I am pleased," said the monk, unexpectedly. Many Thais have been said to be quite successful with the type of training I received and to have gained considerable insight and peace of mind in the process. But Thais have an approach to life, an equanimity, an attitude of mind which is not present in Westerners. Though the methods of meditation I went through may be suited to the Thai mentality, my own opinion is that they are totally unsuited to the Westerner's. Indeed, in my case I feared they may be positively harmful if continued any further.

But to me, as I walked out into the sunshine again, there was this much to be said for my harrowing experiences. They had provided valuable insight into Buddhist practices and thought. And they were to prove useful in shedding light on other experiences which came later in my search.

6

U Ba Khin: A Dynamo with Peace of Mind

A FEW months later I was due to visit Europe on home leave and decided to pursue my interest further by stopping en route in Burma and India to seek out various religious leaders there. I booked in at the Strand Hotel in Rangoon and went to call on a monk at a Buddhist temple I'd heard about which was offering meditation courses similar to the grueling experience I had undergone in Bangkok. We had a long talk on various aspects of Buddhism and meditation but I made it clear I was not prepared to attempt this method again. I felt it just didn't suit my temperament.

A day or so later at the hotel I met a Burmese who told me of a meditation center led by a prominent government official who had surprising success in teaching foreigners insight meditation.

I was intrigued to learn that a layman and not a monk was active in teaching meditation and decided to pay him a visit and see for myself how he went about it. His name was U Ba Khin. I made arrangements to call on this man and found him to be indeed an unusual person.

In addition to his voluntary and quite time-consuming activities as a teacher of meditation at the center I discovered he was also a very senior and respected government official. He was chairman of Burma's State Agricultural Marketing Board, Accountant General and a personal adviser to the Prime Minister. His accomplishments, competence, efficiency and integrity as a civil servant certainly were evidence of the fruits of the meditation he practiced and taught.

U Ba Khin was a short stocky man with a round face, crew cut, a twinkle in his eyes and an extremely sharp mind. His output of work in his government positions, I learned, could hardly be matched by twenty good men. Arriving at his office in the morning he would attack his duties with enormous vigor. When he found himself getting fatigued he would adopt the lotus attitude in a specially designed chair at his desk, meditate for a few minutes to purge his mind and body of accumulated toxins, developed from the strain of the pace he kept up, then immediately return to work. It was his practice to continue this procedure throughout the day, thus demonstrating at least to an uninitiated onlooker like me some of the practical applications of meditation in everyday life.

For an elderly man—and he was in his seventies when I met him—he was a powerhouse of dynamic energy, sleeping only a few hours each day and dividing his time between government duties and his work at the meditation center. Here indeed, I thought, was a man who set a clear example that the teachings of Buddhism had something extraordinary to offer.

The meditation center stood on a little hill in the heart of Rangoon's Golden Valley district which was formerly the residential area of British colonial officialdom. The first glimpse one got was of a small golden-spired pagoda. Unlike most Burmese pagodas, however, this was not a solid structure; its central chamber was a shrine room and there were eight smaller wedge shaped rooms surrounding this central shrine.

The small separate rooms were for the use of the students to practice meditation. The center chamber was used by the teacher to monitor the activities of the students and to offer them guidance when needed. Doors connected the center chamber to the meditation rooms so that the teacher and students were able to communicate easily. On the outer walls of the meditation chambers were further doors used by students for entering and leaving the rooms.

I found that a course lasted ten days and was under the personal direction of a teacher who geared the training to the particular needs and capacities of individual students whether they came from East or West.

At the beginning of every course each trainee took a vow of loyalty to the Buddha and his teaching and undertook to be completely obedient to the wishes of the teacher. In addition he had to promise to refrain from stealing, telling lies, indulging in sexual activity, and taking intoxicating drugs or liquor during the time he was at the training center. The trainees had to refrain from eating after twelve noon; simple sleeping quarters and vegetarian meals were supplied free of charge.

The environment and the approach had an immediate appeal for me and having come so far and met the remarkable U Ba Khin himself I committed myself to the ten-day course with enthusiasm—too much enthusiasm as it turned out.

The routine was exacting by Western standards but much more liberal I gathered, than that to be found in most meditation centers in the East. The teacher felt good health was a prerequisite of successful meditation. Trainees rose at four each morning, meditated from 4:30 to 6 a.m. Breakfast was at 6 a.m. followed by meditation from 7:30 to 10:30.

The last meal of the day was then taken, followed by afternoon meditation between 12:30 and 5 p.m. Then there was one hour for rest and relaxation followed by an informal talk by the teacher and evening meditation between 7 p.m. and 9 p.m. At 9 p.m. the trainees retired for the night.

The training followed the classic Buddhist tradition and consisted of three parts: sīla, or morality; samādhi, or concentration developed by attention to the breath; and paññā, or wisdom developed through the practice of vipassanā.

Sīla

First I found there was a very good reason for the vegetarian diet of two meals a day. Light, wholesome, balanced meals are easier to digest and better assimilated and keep the body, and therefore the mind, from becoming sluggish. It takes hard physical labour to burn up the elements contained in beef, pork, pastries and sweets. If the body does not burn them up through activity they become a dross and begin to burn up the body.

The rule prohibiting alcohol and drugs also had sound reasons. Drugs and alcohol are depressants and a clean, clear mind is essential to proper concentration. Recent studies on sleep have shown that dreams play an essential role in the proper functioning of the mind. Electroencephalograph studies of people sleeping have enabled researchers to know when a person is dreaming. A person deprived of this dream sleep can develop increased anxiety, become highly irritable, and experience difficulty in concentrating. Some show temporary personality changes, becoming impulsive and even paranoid.

Barbiturates, tranquilizers and alcohol all produce abnormalities in dreaming and interfere with the normal dream processes of releasing repressed aggressions and hostilities. Any factors, therefore, which could cause a malfunctioning of the mind were wisely eliminated.

SAMĀDHI

The practice of concentration demands patience, persistence and endurance, just how much only those who have attempted to practise it can know.

There are a number of techniques used by Buddhists, Christians, Hindus, Yogis and other meditators in practicing meditation. The beginner at the Center was taught to concentrate on the breath as it enters and leaves the nostrils. In doing this he must be tireless in excluding all other thoughts and at the same time learn to relax his body and gradually focus the attention until he is only aware of a tiny spot at the base of the nose. Little by little all conscious awareness of breathing stops and he is aware only of a minute point of light and warmth.

It is essential that he develops this attention to a single powerful lens of concentration for without this he can never hope to attain wisdom or insight. The mind can thus become keenly awake, crystal clear, free from dross and ready to experience wisdom which comes to him intuitively

PAÑÑĀ

The practice of vipassanā, the heart of meditation, the means by which insight and wisdom are attained, is something to be experienced rather than described. No amount of intellectual discourse or academic study can substitute for it. The attainment of a crystal clear mind through samādhi is a necessary prerequisite to vipassanā, the understanding of the Four Noble Truths of Buddhism and the nature of anicca, dukkha, and anattā, before one can free oneself from desire and be released from suffering.

I completed the ten-day course at the center but my enthusiasm to learn let me down. I spent a good part of my time analyzing, speculating, making copious notes, and in my zeal I'm afraid I missed the whole object of the exercise.

U Ba Khin saw this and went to great lengths to get me to come down to a less lofty plane. I struck up a friendship with another of the trainees, a psychiatrist from Los Angeles, California, whose wife had previously taken the course with such profound effect that the psychiatrist had put aside his notepad and couch and come out to Rangoon determined to experience a similar "awakening" himself.

The impressive change he had seen in his wife was so remarkable that he concluded meditation had something to offer which science had so far missed. He dedicated himself to find out what it was. Like me, he was researching, looking for something, analyzing and probing. We were both missing the point completely and, seeing this, U Ba Khin did everything he could to separate us.

I don't know what became of the poor psychiatrist; I left with an excellent intellectual comprehension of the process but was so involved in a desire to understand that the very desire prevented full understanding.

Unfortunately my search for understanding was to continue some time before I was able to return to the basic and simple requirements to transcend my inquisitive mind.

I left the meditation center run by U Ba Khin much wiser in the techniques of Buddhism and very impressed by the sage himself. Here was a good man in the real sense of the word. A gentle, quietly spoken and humorous teacher of a faith which possessed the means of solving some of humanity's problems, but which above all was a personal faith which, followed devoutly and practiced assiduously, could arm its adherents against the difficulties which life presents to the individual.

In the short time I spent with him I came to know U Ba Khin as a simple teacher, a profound thinker, a lover of beauty. He was passionately fond of orchids and there were thousands of these graceful flowers in the gardens of the meditation center. I had found that, to him, beauty, compassion, spiritual peace, truth, morality and so on were not just words, nor were they an end in themselves. They were a way of life, part of his very existence.

❈

I decided to carry out a little investigation into the man himself, the guru and the accountant, the high priest of Buddhism and the high civil servant and confidant of his country's Prime Minister. What I found confirmed for me that in my somewhat ill-planned and haphazard search for truth and the meaning of the "quiet mind" I had stumbled on a truly remarkable personality.

U Ba Khin 1889-1971

Since his retirement from full-time government service in 1953 he seemed to have held more senior posts than most ordinary men hold during their active careers. At one time he was holding three separate sanctional appointments of the status of head of a department for nearly three years, and on another occasion four such posts simultaneously for about a year. In addition U Ba Khin held a number of special assignments either as a member of standing committees in the department of Prime Minister or as chairman or member of ad hoc committees. He was made Director of Commercial Audit, Chairman of the State Agricultural Marketing Board and principal of the Government Institute for Accounts and Audit, which he himself helped to establish for the purpose of giving training to the officers and staff of all the Boards and Corporations in Burma.

At one stage, as Director of Commercial Audit, he was required by the Prime Minister to investigate irregularities suspected in the State Agricultural Marketing Board and subsequent reports made by him as chairman of the S.A.M.B. special inquiry committee led to the arrest of four officers of the Board, including the general manager.

It was in the unsettled atmosphere following this incident that he was offered, and accepted, the Board's chairmanship and the events that ensued illustrated well the man's capacity for leadership and talent as an organizer of large-scale State undertakings.

Here was no idle dreamer, no vague philosopher who walked apart from other men rapt in his own thoughts. This was an intensely practical worker, a man who got things done, a man who might have had a notice pinned up behind his desk declaring "The buck stops here," or the appropriate Burmese equivalent.

I was able to read a number of official documents relating to U Ba Khin's responsibilities in Government service, including reports and annual accounts of the departments with which he was concerned as chairman. All of them gave a convincing picture of growth, productivity and success under his guidance. Efficiency, drive, tireless application, clarity of purpose seemed to be his watchwords.

A casual glance at U Ba Khin's record of achievements in office shows them to be remarkable, even phenomenal. How did he do it? The answer is found in the words of Lun Baw, chairman of the Public Service Commission of the Union of Burma. When Mr. Ben Gurion, Prime Minister of Israel, visited Burma in 1961, U Ba Khin addressed a meeting of Israeli Press representatives and what he said was published later in booklet form. In a preface Lun Baw wrote:

"A man who has undergone courses of Buddhist meditation is able to make quick decisions, correct and sound judgment and concerted effort—mental capabilities which definitely contribute to success in life. And at the same time, by the same process of purification of mind, the physical body becomes automatically cleansed and physical fitness is ensured. To attain these objectives the correct method or technique of meditation is essential.

"Herein lies the simple and yet efficient technique of U Ba Khin."

7

"A Sort of Philosopher"

I LEFT Burma for India well pleased with what I had learned and experienced but distinctly disappointed that my nature did not permit me to benefit fully from the training given at U Ba Khin's meditation center. I had taken a step further in my search and had reaped certain psychological rewards, but it was not enough. I was still a long way from achieving what I had set out to achieve.

Before I departed from the center I wrote the following words as my personal testimonial to the place and its remarkable leading light: "The Karmic forces that led me to you and your inspiring guidance have made on me an indelible impression of the light of the Dhamma. The center, the people associated with the center, and Guruji U Ba Khin can only command first place among my memories."

Professors, university lecturers, doctors, a missile research engineer, a film director, even an Ambassador to Burma, were among those who also had expressed their feelings in writing on the apparently wondrous results of a course at the center. I read their words of praise with growing frustration and impatience with myself that such wonders had proved to be so near to hand yet just beyond my reach.

In India I began searching for various religious leaders, gurus, yogis and so-called enlightened ones. I visited Tibetan monks in Sikkim, Hindu teachers and yogis in Calcutta, Benares, Delhi, Rishikesh, Madras and Bombay, and Buddhist monks in Bodh Gaya.

I saw and spoke to teachers in many parts of India, discussed with them their various systems of mind and body control and entered into an assortment of strange practices, some of which I will describe, but none of which I found produced anything more than a temporary, trancelike state through repetition of words, chanting or concentration upon neutral objects.

Many of the experiments brought on in me a certain calm but I was still totally unable to transcend the activities of a mischievous and probing mind. I felt I knew the reason for my failure, as I have explained before, but how could I search for light without dedicating my mental faculties wholly to the search? How could I perceive the truth without consciously and devotedly looking for it? It was like playing hide and seek with my own shadow.

While waiting for my plane to take of off at Benares for New Delhi I noticed an Indian taking his leave of a group of friends. He was a striking figure, getting on in years—perhaps in his late sixties—tall, with a full head of greying hair. He was dressed in the familiar simple lightweight suit of white linen. His departure was evidently the cause of some sorrow to his friends, who were earnestly wishing him a safe journey and urging him to return soon. I concluded he was same kind of celebrity or honored guest.

We went up the steps of the plane together and I was soon in my seat and deep in a book I had purchased at the airport bookstall, unconscious of my surroundings except for the fact that a good-looking young American woman settled down in the seat next to me.

I paid no further attention to the man in the white suit and indeed forgot about him for the rest of that leg of the journey. I noticed an odd thing, however. Perhaps it was of no significance but the man carried no luggage with him.

The plane made a stop at Lucknow. The passengers alighted and we all went into the airport lounge to be served with lunch. I noticed that the Europeans gravitated to a table together and my first inclination was to join them. I changed my mind, however, when I saw the elderly man whom I had seen earlier go towards a smaller table at which the only other occupant was an Indian Army officer. I was in India, after all, to meet Indians and this would be a good chance to acquire a taste of local color. We exchanged the usual cordialities and I sat down. I introduced myself and he told me his name was Krishnamurti. "I am a sort of philosopher," he said.

Had I known at that moment what I was to learn later about Krishnamurti I might have been awed with the significance of the occasion. For this was my first encounter with a man who for over forty years has held thousands all over the world spellbound with his wisdom, a teacher revered not only in his native India but in Europe and the United States too; a man who in his youth was groomed for stardom by well-meaning people as the Messiah reborn, no less.

I knew nothing of this: he was a fellow passenger on the plane and we had met by chance over the lunch table. At first our conversation was general. We talked about the weather, war and all the usual topics. He asked if I'd pass the salt. We were offered a choice of meat or vegetarian dishes and he chose the vegetarian diet. As a matter of interest and to make conversation I asked him why he had opted for the salad and he replied that he simply preferred the food, there was no particular moral principle involved. Like many Indians he had been brought up on vegetarian foods and the preference had stayed with him.

Knowing that Krishna was an Indian word meaning "God" I ventured to ask him what was the meaning of his name, Krishnamurti. It is customary in Southern India for the eighth child, if a boy, to be named after Krishna and his name, he told me with no trace of self-consciousness, meant "in the likeness of God." From this point our conversation began to veer away from the commonplace chitchat of fellow airplane passengers and I felt, if not actually encouraged, not actively discouraged, to go a stage further. As we both had some time on our hands I could see no harm in developing the conversation and there was, in any case, something about the man, an indefinable quality, an aura, which seemed to invite questions and in some strange way guarantee that his answers would be worth hearing. I would chance it, anyway.

"You say you are a 'sort of philosopher' yet, knowing the meaning of your name, I should say you are a religious man also," I suggested.

"If by that you mean do I follow a religion the answer would be 'no', sir," he said. "Nor do I follow any particular philosophy. I believe all philosophies and religions are wrong. The spoken or written word is not the truth. Truth can only be experienced directly at the moment it happens. Any thought or intellectual projection of the truth is a step away from the truth, sir."

I paused for a moment to try and take in what he had said. He spoke quickly and directly in an impeccable Oxford accent; and I could not help being amused, if a little embarrassed, by the way he addressed me formally as "sir" although I was a mere twenty-eight to his sixty-five or more. I could see the Indian Army officer at our table was more than a little surprised at the turn our conversation was taking but, rather rudely maybe, I paid no attention to him and he went on with his meal in silence.

"Since you don't follow any of the established religions," I asked, "which of the great religious leaders came closest to teaching and realizing the ultimate truth?"

"Oh, the Buddha," replied Krishnamurti without hesitation and somewhat to my astonishment. I had expected him to mention one of the Indian gods or even Christ. "The Buddha comes closer to the basic truths and facts of life than any other. Although I am not myself a Buddhist, of course."

"Why not?" I asked, as politely as possible to make up for my directness.

"No organization, however old or however recent, can lead a man to truth. It is a hindrance, it can only impede. It blocks a man from sincere study. The truth comes from within, by seeing for yourself. The conventional way of acquiring knowledge, it's true, is by reading or listening but to understand you have to penetrate directly, by silently observing. Then you understand."

He paused and I waited for him to go on. "Obviously if you are going to build a bridge you must study strains and stresses, but in the matter of understanding truth or the concepts of love, philosophical or religious thoughts, anything to do with reality, it has to be penetrated and experienced directly without any intellectual interpretation. Truth comes from within. Once the understanding comes you are able to talk about it but it does not follow that a listener will understand."

"If you described a book or a motor car or the plane we are travelling in I would understand," I said.

"That is the purpose of the intellect, sir—to communicate. Mechanical or materialistic things can be understood, but if I tried to tell you what God is, what truth is or what love is you would not fully understand. Perhaps I know what love is, what God is, what reality is—I could write a book on what love is or what reality is and you could read it and intellectually you would understand the book, but it does not follow automatically that you would know what love is, or what reality is. This you must understand by direct experience, without interpretation and without intellectualization. The thought and the word are not the thing but a distortion of the reality."

The old man's flow of words was entirely fascinating and I became very anxious to continue the discussion. When the meal was finished and our fellow passengers began to move towards the plane once again I asked him if I might occupy the seat next to him and talk further. He seemed glad to have a companion, then a shadow of doubt crossed his face.

"But what about that nice girl you were sitting with before we stopped here? She might be offended if you leave her." His concern for the girl—even the fact that he had noticed her—bewildered me. I didn't know the girl at all and we had exchanged only a few polite sentences. I reassured the old man and moved my baggage to the rack nearest his seat.

"I see you have no bags—you're travelling light," I said.

"I am only going as far as New Delhi," he replied, "I have no need of possessions and carry none. I have no money with me either—I never handle it."

"What will you do without money or clothes in Delhi?" I asked. "How will you manage for food and accommodation?"

"I shall be among friends," he replied simply. "I have been invited to speak and the people who wish me to make speeches also pay for my journey, my food and anything else I require. They also put me up in their homes and you may be certain I shall be comfortable and want for nothing."

"As a matter of fact," he went on, "I have no permanent home or any possessions, I spend my life travelling from place to place and my friends everywhere look after my needs. I belong nowhere, yet everywhere, and my friends are everywhere. My needs are simple."

I think Krishnamurti was amused by my expression of incredulity. It must surely have shown in my face. Even now I did not guess that he was a world renowned mystic with a following in almost every land ready to welcome him on his visits as their spiritual leader. In spite of all my reading and study of Eastern philosophy and religious beliefs I had not encountered the name of Krishnamurti, and for him it must have been something of a novelty to meet such an earnest young man who quite obviously had never heard of him.

I did, however, recognize that I was in the presence of a remarkable personality, a man whose words were getting through to me and meaning something. My search for truth and the quiet mind was at last beginning to show the glimmer of results. Looking back, I think it may have been precisely because I was not one of his admirers that induced Krishnamurti to talk so freely to me. My questioning was unforgivably probing for a complete stranger, yet his answers were detailed and frank and, far from discouraging me or seeming reproachful for my self-confident cross-examination, he seemed to enjoy it and even invite more.

His speech was lively and fluent and the flourishes and gestures that accompanied it were forceful and expressive. The airplane engines droned on monotonously and while other passengers read or slept we conducted our vigorous discussion.

"How do you live?" I asked, returning to his earlier theme.

"Oh, things just happen. I'm well provided for. I am happier without possessions of my own. People give me things but I can take them or leave them. What do we want with possessions? When you don't want things they come to you. When you do want things then you're in conflict and when you don't get them you suffer. When you get them you want something else which causes further suffering. My needs are very simple. All I need is something to eat every day, a few calories, enough clothes to keep me warm. These are very adequately provided for me. The only clothes I own are these I'm wearing," he laughed.

"Man's real needs are simple. And it is quite easy to satisfy them. Television and automobiles are not needed to sustain life and indeed they lead to conflict. When you desire them and devote attention to acquiring them this is where conflict comes into life. You are never satisfied.

"We tend to live in confusion instead of clarity. This is destructive. Out of confusion more confusion grows. But if we are aware of the confusion we can stop and examine. Don't take action out of confusion, sir. Take action based on clarity."

"How can one achieve clarity?"

"We have to understand living, the living of our daily life, with all its misery, confusion, conflict. It is not easy. If we can understand how to live, death is close. Without dying there is no living. We should observe ourselves constantly. See ourselves, our greed, envy, bitterness, cynicism, beliefs—and watch them. We cannot see them if we want to change them. Actual seeing demands energy, active and constant observation."

"How would you answer a person who sought your advice on developing spiritually?" I asked. Krishnamurti's face grew serious.

"Simply by silently watching yourself all the time, all your actions, your thoughts, your environment. Be silently aware of things as they occur, without interpretation.

"But I cannot advise," he said, laughing suddenly. "When people ask me for advice or assurance it is the same as asking for a medicine. I cannot give it. The answer is within themselves. They must look for it. They are seeking security and there is no such thing. That's why they believe in a religion or try to reach God—it's the desire to feel safe. A man is his own salvation and it is only through himself that he will find the truth, not through religions, thoughts or theories, and certainly not through following a leader. Leaders and followers exploit each other and I will have nothing to do with such activities!

"It's because of this urge to feel safe that we put our faith in leaders. And why? Because we don't want to do the wrong thing. Fear, not clarity, is the basis of following. We want a permanent idea, a permanent God. When clarity is come to we don't want to follow. My teaching does not involve faith, but a mind that is free to examine."

"Is there, then, no value in following a religion?" I asked.

"All organized religions are forms of escape, sir. They offer comfort, tell you what to do. If you behave properly you will be rewarded. It is childish. It is a block to understanding."

There were many more questions I felt I must put to this sage old Indian whose words had struck, for the first time, a chord of true response in my mind. But the changing note of the engines indicated that, all too soon, the journey was over and in a few minutes we would land and go our separate ways.

"Shall we meet in Delhi?" I asked.

"I shall be gone in a few days," he replied.

"Where are you going next?"

"America, perhaps, or Switzerland," he said vaguely. "I prefer a mild climate, you know."

As he rose to leave the plane I noticed for the first time that he carried a book under his arm. When he saw me glance at the title he smiled a little sheepishly. "This is the only kind of literature I read. Everything else bores me."

It was a paperback crime thriller.

I collected my bags and headed for the airport buildings and the door marked "exit." I turned but there was no sign of the man in the white linen suit—I saw only the crowd of excited men and women, and the press photographers, who had Krishnamurti somewhere in their midst.

8

Into the Tent, Out of the Rain

MY first meeting with Krishnamurti and our illuminating conversation on the flight to New Delhi took place in 1958. Although I have been privileged to meet and talk with him on a number of occasions since then there was for several years never the same rapport, the same free flowing exchange of question and answer. Each subsequent meeting has, nonetheless, been rewarding in its way and my pursuit of the ultimate truth, which by now had become a consuming passion, gained fresh impetus as a result of them.

But who was Krishnamurti? What was his background?

I was on my way to the States and my next stop after Delhi was Paris, where I had some time on my hands before taking the long transatlantic hop home. The words of Krishnamurti were still sounding in my ears as I searched the bookshops along the Left Bank for more reading material on the general subject of Eastern religions and philosophies.

It was with surprise and delight, therefore, that I spotted two books written by Krishnamurti and another that told the story of his life. With the aid of these books and talks I had with other interested people I met in Paris I was able to piece together the man's extraordinary progress through life.

He was born in 1897 at Madanapalle in Madras, the son of a revenue clerk who worked for the British Government. His mystical qualities were recognized by the theosophist Mrs. Annie Besant, who first noticed the lad playing on the beach near his home with his brother. Mrs. Besant and her colleague C. W. Leadbeater saw in him faculties which, if properly developed, could make him a great spiritual leader. They drew the boy's father's attention to what they believed and arranged to adopt Krishnamurti, promising to give him the education needed to fulfill the boy's destiny.

The father, who was a poor man, accepted the situation cheerfully and allowed Mrs. Besant to take the youngster and his younger brother into her care. She took the boys to Europe and announced publicly that the young Krishnamurti possessed latent greatness which would be revealed to the world in due course. Thus, from the age of fourteen, the boy became a subject of curiosity and a public figure. He went to school in England while thousands of theosophists waited for his emergence as their leader. An international organization named "The Order of the Star" was formed to pave the way for his coming, and it accumulated vast funds and property, in readiness for the supreme work he was to do.

Krishnamurti's father became alarmed at what was happening and tried unsuccessfully to get his son returned to him. There was a sensational law suit but Mrs. Besant secured her guardianship and Krishnamurti's education for the special task ordained for him went ahead. When he spoke at a meeting in Holland before 6,000 people Annie Besant declared that there rang out a voice not heard on earth for 2,000 years.

Then his brother, Nityananda, died. Krishnamurti watched him dying and his grief was intense, but out of the tragic experience came an inspiration that put the seal on his future as a spiritual teacher and at the same time raised doubts in his mind on his mission as the returned Messiah.

He wrote: "When my brother died the experience it brought me was great—not only the sorrow, sorrow is momentary and passes away—but the joy of experience remains. If you understand life rightly, then death becomes an experience out of which you can build your house of perfection, your house of delight."

From that moment the young Krishnamurti realized what his true destiny was to be and he embarked on his life's work which was to show all men how to attain the supreme and lasting happiness which he had found within himself. On the day, in 1929, when he was to be proclaimed as the new Messiah he stood up in front of his excited and expectant audience and deliberately renounced the role elaborately prepared for him. He dissolved the "Order of the Star" and rejected the worldwide organization which had been built up around him. He told his astonished listeners: "I desire those who seek to understand me to be free. Truth is a pathless land and you cannot approach it by any path whatsoever, by any religion, by any sect."

Thus emerged a deeply individual thinker and leader of thought whose philosophy of life was in close harmony with modern conditions. As he developed he became more and more firmly convinced— as he was to explain to me on that memorable plane journey some thirty-five years later—that organized religions merely presented a barrier to progress in the search for truth, throwing up useless and obstructive distinctions.

Through the years since that turning point in Krishnamurti's life he has traveled the world, speaking where he was asked to speak, helping with spiritual counsel where his help was sought, but always rejecting the role of a world teacher, repudiating any suggestion that his teaching was going to heal the world's ills or form the basis of a religion which would prove to be man's salvation.

For me the essence of his message is contained in a foreword to one of his books. His friend Aldous Huxley, at whose home, he told me, he stays sometimes, wrote: "There is a transcendent spontaneity of life, a creative reality which reveals itself as immanent only when the perceiver's mind is in a state of alert passivity, of choiceless awareness." Krishnamurti himself, when we met again four years later, showed me in simple terms how he saw this happening:

"Maybe, one day, while I am delivering one of my talks in a tent or shelter, it will be raining outside and someone walking down the street, someone who has never heard of me, will walk into the tent to get out of the rain. Perhaps in such a situation of spontaneity that man will understand what I am saying."

So far I have told the story of my search in chronological sequence, describing events in the order in which they occurred. During the years immediately following my first meeting with Krishnamurti, however, I met him again on a number of occasions and frequently listened to his talks before audiences in various parts of the world where our paths chanced to cross. I will therefore add at this point a few brief notes on incidents which arose out of these subsequent encounters because they help to explain the man and his message.

That he was a remarkable personality and a profound teacher and thinker I was in no doubt at all. As a philosopher he was irresistible—but that's not to say I necessarily understood every word he uttered—and his personal magnetism was unique in my experience. Back in Thailand, four years after our first meeting, I heard that Krishnamurti was scheduled to give a series of lectures in India. I wrote to an address in New Delhi for dates and places when he would be likely to appear and decided that at the first opportunity, as work permitted, I would go to Delhi to hear him.

Krishnamurti was staying at the home of Mrs. Kitty Shiva Rao, an Austrian woman who was married to an Indian member of Parliament. On my arrival in Delhi I wrote to her requesting a personal interview and was rewarded with a polite reply inviting me to lunch the next day. I went along at the appointed time and was greeted warmly and with perhaps some natural curiosity by the lady of the house.

I had fully expected to be summarily refused the interview I wanted. Krishnamurti, a world figure with an enormous following, was doubtless glad of any opportunity to relax out of the company of the listeners and questioners who trailed in his footsteps and it was certainly beyond my expectations that he should wish to put up with the likes of me during lunch. I thought he would at least expect to take his meals in peace.

When we met and shook hands my first reaction was one of shock. He seemed to have aged several years since our meeting on the plane. For a while I could not be sure he remembered me, though he said he did, asked me where I had been and what I had been doing. I told him about the places I had visited since our last meeting and of my quest for the secret of a quiet mind.

"What about you?" I asked. "Where have you been?"

"Oh, just about everywhere," he said, a smile playing around his tired eyes. "I don't remember exactly all the places I have visited. The only countries I have not been to yet are Russia and China."

He asked me if I had read his books *The First and Last Freedom* and *Commentaries on Living*. I said I had found these in a secondhand bookshop in Paris and read them with interest.

"They describe my views and thoughts," he said. "I thought you would find them useful if you really were interested in what we talked about last time."

I said I had read those books and others. They propounded an unusual philosophy, one which was not guided by the teaching of any of the accepted prophets and indeed even rejected them.

He laughed and his unwrinkled face creased up. "That's true. I'm a rebel. I learned early in life that religions are not the way to happiness, to truth. You can only achieve these by direct experience. You must look for the truth yourself and find it for yourself. Leaders and followers exploit each other. That is not the path to happiness. I tell people 'Don't believe me—look to yourself.'"

We joined Mr. and Mrs. Shiva Rao and sat down for lunch. The dining room was cool and the food, partly Indian, partly European, was delicious and exquisitely cooked. The conversation covered most of the usual topics. We talked about our travels, my counterespionage work in SE Asia, and Indian and American politics; we even talked about sex, the new permissive society, teenagers and modern "pop" music and I found Krishnamurti knowledgeable in the most unlikely subjects. He clearly had kept his eyes open on his journeys. Despite all the forms of entertainment available to young people nowadays he doubted whether they were really happy. Their folly, he thought, was that they did not seek happiness within themselves but were content to depend on others to make them happy; they followed the rules of current convention and preferred to be led rather than to seek for themselves.

After lunch Krishnamurti and I moved into another room where, said the kindly Mrs. Shiva Rao, we could talk without interruption. If I had felt something of an intruder when I had first entered her house she had done everything possible to make me feel at ease.

I had a list of questions to which I hoped the sage would give me his answers. It would serve no purpose to give a verbatim account here of this private discussion since, if Krishnamurti's doctrine is worth anything at all, an individual's questions are answerable only by the individual himself and nothing would be gained by his sitting in on a recital of mine. It would, furthermore, be churlish of me to set down in cold print words spoken to me in confidence. I have no misgivings, however, about giving a summarized version of a significant part of our talk.

"Since you do not acknowledge any religious leader because religion itself acts as a barrier, why do you give lectures all over the world and what do you try to put across in them?" I asked.

"Words cannot communicate experience to another," he replied. "I can only help my listeners to discover and examine the obstacles in the way of such experience and thus remove them by the very awareness of their causes and effects. I do not offer conclusions but experiences, and invite my listeners to drop their preconceived ideas and attack their problems directly and anew."

"Can 'transcendental' meditation help in this?" I asked.

"In the ordinary state we have the observer and the observed," he said. "We have duality, and where there's duality there's conflict. In the transcendental state the observer and the observed become one. There is no longer duality, there's bliss. The thinker and the thought are one. The experiencing of 'what is' without naming it brings about freedom from what is."

"We live in a practical world," I said. "Surely a person reaching this state of bliss would turn into a vegetable, unable to cope with life as it has to be lived."

"On the contrary," said Krishnamurti. "Such a person would be capable of true and creative action with love."

He gave an example of a large stone lying in the middle of the road and how different people would react to a situation which could give rise to danger for passing motorists.

"One person may ignore the stone for it is not inconvenient to him. Another person, noticing his friends watching from a distance, would pick up the stone hoping his friends would think highly of him. Yet another passer-by would remove the stone of his own accord and think highly of himself. There is another kind of person still, who would remove the stone through pure action, without any motive, simply because the stone didn't belong in the middle of the road."

Krishnamurti's presence is striking. This said, it is hard to pinpoint just why. I have already attempted to describe his magnetism. One writer has called him a living paradox, by which I understand a mass of contradictions.

He laughs easily, but as easily grows serious; he will be whimsical one minute and grave the next. His light complexion made me think at first he was Kashmirian, yet he was born in Southern India. He has deep brown eyes which are the most expressive I have seen. They can smoulder, blaze, twinkle in humour, penetrate with a glance or glaze over to give you the feeling that although he is looking at you he does not see you.

He can seem to be unkind to a questioner and his patience seems to run out sometimes yet I have heard him vehemently deny this. In a certain mood or reaction to a situation he will raise his head in a lofty attitude of authority but he claims no authority and indeed, though an outstandingly learned man, insists that he does not presume to teach or aspire to lead.

I left the Shiva Rao house believing that if I had ever encountered a saint in my travels it was that afternoon, for a saintlier person than Krishnamurti it would be hard to meet. I tried to decide what I meant by a saint. An enlightened person? He is surely one of the most enlightened individuals in the world today. A person who knows God—or knows he is God? We may all be said to be manifestations of God without realizing it; perhaps he is one who does.

One who is not in conflict? Surely a person who is free from conflict, free from illusions, who is united with God in the mystical way that Krishnamurti is united must be some kind of saint.

A moving example of the paradox of Krishnamurti occurred at Benares when I was paying a visit to a school founded on his principles. He goes there from time to time to speak to the children but on this occasion the hall was filled with youngsters and grown-ups.

While we waited for his arrival we heard President Kennedy had been assassinated—an announcement was made from the stage. There were cries of disbelief and shock at the news, sobbing broke out among young and old alike and it was clear the tragedy had an immediate effect of gloom in that small corner of the world as it had everywhere else.

When Krishnamurti appeared and began his talk it was as if nothing had happened. He proceeded with the discussion planned and spoke for an hour without mentioning a word about the appalling happening in Dallas.

Was this callous? Did his studied disregard of the Kennedy murder show a heartless lack of feeling? I knew his views about leaders, political or religious. "Fear is the basis of following, not clarity," he had said to me. "It is because of the urge to feel safe that we put our faith in leaders."

But I could also recall his words on life and death. "If we can understand how to live, death is close. Without dying there is no living."

Since I don't claim to be more than averagely enlightened I cannot vouch for the veracity of my interpretation of these words, but as I sat in the school hall at Benares surrounded by Indians and a few Europeans to whom Kennedy's violent death was a staggering blow I could not help reflecting that it was completely in character for Krishnamurti to register not the slightest emotion. Death is part of life. And why should any part of life be a subject for, or inducement to, grief? I was as affected by the event as the weeping woman sitting in the chair next to mine, but this was surely just another manifestation of the conflict in which we experience life. Krishnamurti knows no conflict.

Krishnamurti thoroughly dislikes being photographed, though later he was to allow me the privilege of taking a snapshot of him for this book. I was present on one occasion when I feared an unpleasant incident might develop. It was during one of his lectures in India. A number of tourists were among the audience and at one point, while Krishnamurti was in full voice, a Japanese stood up and aimed his camera at the speaker.

"Stop!" cried Krishnamurti.

The Japanese was nonplussed and very embarrassed at what he obviously felt was an intrusion on the tourist's prerogative, but Krishnamurti was clearly quite agitated. I wondered why.

Afterwards, when we were alone, I brought up the subject of the innocent photographer who had merely tried to add a picture of Krishnamurti to his holiday record. He told me he never allowed photographs if he could help it because he was afraid some people might misuse them. There were those who wished to deify him and pictures would give them a means of doing so. The thought horrified him. He even knew people who would build temples around him as they did for Buddha and Christ.

"This is precisely what should not be done," he emphasized. "It only takes you further from the truth. It is a distraction."

J. Krishnamurti 1895-1986

Krishnamurti's mission is to guide, but it is the guidance and not the guide which is important. "I am a signpost," he once said.

He is certainly the most unself-conscious of signposts, and the least publicity conscious. He wanders about the world unheralded, unadvertised, unpublicized. He has no press agent, no public relations machinery to propagate his message. He rarely gives interviews for newspapers or radio and so far as I know has never been seen on television. He speaks, takes a plane, arrives, speaks again. If his audience listens he is pleased but he has scant hope that all of them will understand his words.

I have heard him speak in many parts of the world and before a variety of audiences. I have noticed the same faces among his audiences, because there are people who follow him around the world. Wealthy dowagers some of them, I suspect, who have more money than they know what to do with. They gaze in awe at Krishnamurti as he speaks. They have heard it all before, yet they don't understand a word of what he's saying. "One day perhaps someone will understand me," he told me, when I mentioned this to him.

Why does he speak? He gave this answer as long ago as 1929: "As an artist paints a picture, because he takes delight in painting, because it is his self-expression, his glory, his whole being, so I do this and not because I want anything from anyone."

Krishnamurti's message is that one must look to oneself for the truth, for enlightenment. I believe his talks often are hard to understand, even impossible, because he intends them to be that way, so the listener will look inward at himself. "Don't believe me—look to yourself for the truth."

I believe he sometimes deliberately leads his listeners nowhere, frustrates them to the point where they seek the answers within themselves. He advocates the quiet mind, the quiet and alert mind.

I fixed up an appointment to meet him at Benares on one occasion and he agreed to see me. I prepared a list of questions which were relevant to my inquiries at the time. When we met he did not remember me at all, or seemed not to, and there was practically no communication between us. He gave no answers, or answered in a way that meant nothing to me, and in the end I walked away bitterly disappointed. Then I realized the lesson I had learned was clearer than if we had talked for two hours.

As I read through Krishnamurti's books I became totally engrossed in the messages he conveyed: alert passivity, "silent awareness," "the thinker and the thought are one," "the experiencing of what is without naming it brings about freedom from what is." Almost every word he uttered was reminiscent of the understanding brought about through "transcendental" meditation.

❧

At a private interview in 1967—it was at the Shiva Rao house again—I raised with him the questions of pain and pleasure and the place of suffering in the human condition, and of desire and the pursuit of pleasure. "When there is pleasure there is also pain," he said. "Pleasure and pain go together as one."

I asked: "What happens when there's no pleasure—is there pain?"

"That's a very good question," he replied. "Now look at that. When there is no pleasure and no pain what do you have? Watch that, watch that very carefully and see what there is." He was talking about the transcendental state.

❧

It was almost eleven years after my first meeting with Krishnamurti, after I had settled for a two-year stay in England, that I heard about Brockwood Park and the Krishnamurti Foundation.

News reached me that, from funds contributed by his followers, an organization had been set up with the object of providing a center for the furtherance of his work. It had purchased a country mansion of beautiful proportions set deep in the Hampshire countryside mid-way between Winchester and Petersfield some sixty-five miles from London. Here the teacher, now well into his seventies, would spend an increasing amount of his time between journeys abroad. Talks would be held there and a school would be started for youngsters over the normal school-leaving age, which at the moment in Britain is fifteen.

I wrote off for details and said I would like to motor down and have a look round and perhaps have an hour or two with Krishnamurti or at least attend one of his gatherings. With the reply came two copies of the Foundation's news bulletin, a neatly duplicated pocket-sized booklet containing information about the group's plans and their progress to date and, in one of them, a picture of Brockwood itself, an imposing white-painted building dating from the eighteenth century.

Also in one of the bulletins was this extract from the notebook of Krishnamurti, and I quote it in full because it seems to me to say in a few words all that I have learned from this great man over the years.

"Meditation in which any form of effort is involved ceases to be meditation. It is not an achievement, a thing that is practiced daily according to any system or method to gain a desired end. There must be an end to all imagination and measure. Meditation is not a means to an end: it is an end in itself. But the meditator must come to an end for meditation to be.

"Meditation is not an experience, a memory gathered for a future pleasure. The experiencer always travels within the limits of his own projections of time and thought. Within the boundaries of thought, freedom is an idea, a formula, and the thinker can never come upon the movement of meditation. A movement has no beginning and no ending; but to the thinker there is always the center.

"Meditation is always the present, and thought always belongs to the past. All consciousness is thought, and the state of meditation is not within its boundaries. Conscious meditation is to define more and more the boundaries and to destroy all freedom; within the frontiers of the mind there is no freedom. In freedom alone is there meditation.

"If there is no meditation you are a slave for ever to time, whose shadow is sorrow. Time is sorrow.

"There is no silence without love. Be still, to understand.

"To meditate is to be vulnerable—the vulnerability which has no past and no future, the yesterday and the tomorrow. Only the new is vulnerable.

"Meditation is not the way of unique and exceptional experiences. Such experiences lead to isolation, to the self-enclosing processes of time-binding memories, denying freedom.

"The valley was carpeted with flowers; there was on the slopes a patch of flowers of every color imaginable; and they were abundant— as abundant as the earth itself with its cities, factories, rivers, woods and green meadows. They were there, as rich and beautiful as that valley. But the abundance of nature and man is on the surface of the land, to die and be put together again. The abundance of meditation is not put together by thought or by pleasure that thought breeds; it is on the other side of the flowers and the clouds. From there the abundance is immeasurable, as love and beauty; but they are never on this side of the flowers and the clouds.

"Time is memory. Ecstasy is timeless. The bliss of meditation has no duration. Joy becomes pleasure when it has continuity. The bliss in meditation is only a second by the watch, but in that second is the whole movement of life without time, a movement without a beginning and an end. In meditation the second is the infinite.

"Be far away. Far away from the world of chaos and misery, live in it, untouched. This is only possible when you have a meditative mind, a mind that looks out from behind the flower and the cloud. The meditative mind is unrelated to the past and to the future and yet is sanely capable of living with clarity and reason in this world. The world is disorder and the order of this world is disorder; and its morality is immorality. The clarity out there is not to be sought and made orderly, to be used for this world. When it is used it becomes darkness. The nature of this clarity is its very emptiness. Because it is empty it is clear; because it is negative it is positive. Be far away, not knowing where you are. There, there is no you and me," (Krishnamurti Foundation, London 1969).

The bulletins gave times and dates of gatherings and on a Saturday soon afterwards I drove down into Hampshire to renew my acquaintance with Krishnamurti. Brockwood, set in beautiful unspoiled countryside of woods and rolling hills, was not easy to find but eventually I located the village of Bramdean and the avenue of copper beeches leading off the main road which I had been directed to look out for.

The house looked out over 36 acres of parkland, gardens with well-trimmed lawns, and attractive clusters of trees. One could well imagine that in other days it had been the country seat of titled English aristocracy, its outbuildings the living quarters of a retinue of grooms, butlers and other servants an estate of this size would need to retain.

On one of the lawns a large marquee had been erected and it was here that Krishnamurti was to address his listeners. They had come from far and wide. Alongside my Morris, when I finally parked it in an area at the back of the house, were Peugeots, Volkswagens, Citroëns, Fiats, Renaults, Opels, Volvos, displaying a variety of European registration plates, as well as many British cars. The company was a truly international one, as I was to find out when I mingled with the crowd.

Krishnamurti, moving about among the people, greeted me with a warm smile. He was dressed in blue jeans and a grey sweater. We went into the house and he led me to a room off the main entrance hall where we sat down for a chat like old friends. He was totally unself-conscious and relaxed and seemed completely unaware of the people outside who had come to soak up the words of truth and light he was shortly to utter.

There were a dozen questions I had lined up to put to him. I asked none of them. Perhaps I had forgotten in the time that had elapsed since our last meeting that you do not go to Krishnamurti for answers. He does not pretend to be a kind of spiritual information bureau dispensing instant salvation to all comers. You go to listen and, if you are lucky, to talk with him.

One of the things that had been on my mind was the apparent paradox of the Krishnamurti Foundation and of Brockwood itself. Had he not, years before, put an end once and for all to any conceptions that he might stand as the head of a spiritual organization? Had he not, with very good reasons, turned his back on the ownership of valuable properties in Europe and the United States which were to be the cornerstones of a religious sect with Krishnamurti as its chief prophet?

Needless to say, I mentioned none of these thoughts. Wasn't it only practical that a man who drew a following from everywhere in the world should have some kind of center of operations? And if his message was so worthwhile and so topical in the modern environment wasn't it only right and appropriate that young people should be able to attend a school where the benefits of his teaching could be shared? And the Foundation itself—was it unreasonable that here should be some organized and businesslike approach to public work of this nature? There is nothing of the high priest about Krishnamurti, no pretentiousness, not even an awareness that he is anything exceptional among men unless it is simply that he understands while most do not.

It would have been unthinkable to say any of this as we sat together at Brockwood that afternoon. My thoughts returned to India and the other places where I had met this unassuming man or joined the gatherings of people to hear him speak. Sitting there in his sweater he might have been one of the crowd who had arrived to listen, except that he was the one without the wrinkles.

We talked about my job and the route I had taken to get to Brockwood. We discussed the way the world was going, and the conversation stayed on this general level until I told him that in England in the previous year twenty million prescriptions had been issued under the National Health Service for sleeping pills and tranquilizers.

"It gives a pretty good indication of the conflicts and tensions people suffer from today," I said.

"And that is because of the dualistic process in which man is trapped," said Krishnamurti. "That is the cause of all those anxieties. If only man would look at himself objectively he would drop these foolish avenues of suffering as he would drop a hot piece of coal."

It is not easy for a man to discard suffering, he explained, because it gives him something to dwell on. There is therefore some pleasure to be derived from the dualistic state and as long as the suffering does not become too bad man will put up with it.

"Pleasure and pain are really one and when this is clearly seen one drops the process of duality and lives in peaceful freedom."

Krishnamurti said he himself does not suffer from conflicts and I believe him. Except for his hair which is now white, he looks half his age.

I asked him whether he thought the people who came to Brockwood were understanding his message.

"Oh I think so—I use very simple language," he said. I pointed out this was a different answer from the one he had given me some time ago in India when I put a similar question to him about the followers who return again and again to hear him. "Ah, it's the application of the principles I speak of which is so difficult," he countered. "The problem is to apply what I say to daily living, and people return from time to time to reinforce what they have gained from previous talks."

I told Krishnamurti I was writing an account of my search for a quiet mind and including the people I had met and the experiences. He seemed delighted at the thought until I mentioned that this meant including him. "Oh, you don't want to put me in it; I'll spoil the book," he cried. I told him that furthermore I wished to take a photograph of him to use as an illustration. He didn't like the idea at all but in the end gave in under pressure. "Yes, yes, if you wish," he said, with good-humored protest in his voice. "But you know I'm not fond of publicity and that's the reason I usually oppose the publication of my photograph."

There were two further points I wanted to raise with Krishnamurti before I left Brockwood. It was not long before that the Maharishi Mahesh Yogi was causing a stir among the young people of the Western world with his meditation teaching. I was making a study of the effects of the sensation he had caused. I asked Krishnamurti whether he thought the Maharishi's system was effective.

"I don't think so," he replied. "It didn't last very long."

I mentioned that experiments were being carried out on certain people with the use of electroencephalograph equipment to induce an alpha rhythm state similar to the condition found in Zen meditation. What did he think?

"Any stupid mind can be thus trained," he said. "But what can they do with this ability?"

Krishnamurti fascinated me. He still does and always will. He is a rare soul, perhaps a saint, who can tell? My dialogues with him were refreshing and enlightening in a way that defies proper description.

I have barely scratched the surface of his teaching here, perhaps "approach to living" is a better phrase, but to me, in the role I had given myself of searcher, analyst and chronicler of the concealed depths of the mind he was an invaluable signpost.

The question was, could I read the wording on the sign?

9

Journey to the Roof of the World

BETTY, Jean, Ed and I were all friends in the same line of business in Bangkok. They had become so accustomed to my preoccupation with Eastern spiritual philosophies, the process of the mind and my search for evidence to support the existence of a state which could truly be called "the quiet mind" that they were even beginning to follow my quest with genuine interest, and not merely the indulgent tolerance of comrades and fellow exiles in a foreign land.

During a particularly hot winter I decided to make a trip to the Himalayan resort town of Darjeeling in Northern India to cool off a little and perhaps carry out some incidental research at the same time. The atmosphere in Bangkok was unbearably oppressive and the idea of a couple of weeks' break quickly caught on; the others leapt at the chance of a sight-seeing tour on the scale I envisaged and we telephoned the air terminal to book seats on the next plane out of town.

We flew over Burma to the squalor of Calcutta and from there Northwest to Patna on the Ganges. At Patna we hired a car and driver to take us on to Bagdogra, and for the next leg of our journey we humped our baggage aboard a quaint mountain train at Siliguri. The "toy" train—two-foot gauge track, three coaches and a baby locomotive—steamed with utmost effort up the winding foothills and amid incredible scenery of dense jungle.

The rail trip lasted about six hours but the discomfort was more than amply compensated by the view from the carriage windows when, after the first few miles, the steep ascent began. The palm trees and jungle were replaced by lustrous green landscapes of terraced tea plantations on the hillsides. The green itself was accentuated by the sharp, bright points of color added by the numerous poinsettias and bougainvillea plants dotted here and there as far as the eye could see.

At Kusseong, roughly halfway on our journey, we caught our first glimpse of the mighty peak of Kanchenjunga. Then, four miles before Darjeeling, our little train puffed to the summit of its strenuous ride at Ghoom where we were 8,000 feet above sea level. From there we sped downhill and dropped 1,000 feet in altitude by the time we reached our destination.

We were already very conscious of the drop in temperature when we arrived in West Bengal and the fascinating English-style town of Darjeeling. Darjeeling, notable as a center of the tea industry, a seat of learning—particularly for the young of the wealthy for there were more boarding schools to the acre than any other town I know—and monument to the British Raj both in the atmosphere of the place and in the architectural styles of its buildings.

We reached Darjeeling in midafternoon and checked in at the Windermere Hotel. The name was incongruously English-sounding yet somehow appropriate for the kind of country in which the town was situated. We were made welcome with exceptional warmth by the genial Tibetan landlord and his lovely smiling wife. Their name was Tenderflower and we liked them at once. They showed us our rooms, which were small but comfortable with hot and cold water laid on and only one small drawback: the heating arrangements seemed a good deal less than adequate. We were finding it difficult to adjust to the cold, sharp air. But the hospitable Tenderflowers did what they could for our comfort and we felt we were in good hands.

When we were unpacked and settled we sat before the big open fire in the bar and sipped hot toddies. Ed complimented our host and hostess on the beauty of the surrounding countryside and told them we had come to savor the coolness of the northern climate and take in some of the local scenery.

"In that case, tomorrow you must go to Tiger Hill," said Tenderflower. It was a renowned beauty spot, he explained, about seven miles north which provided views of the Himalayas no tourist worthy of the name would care to miss.

"We'll certainly have to do that," said Betty enthusiastically. We all agreed.

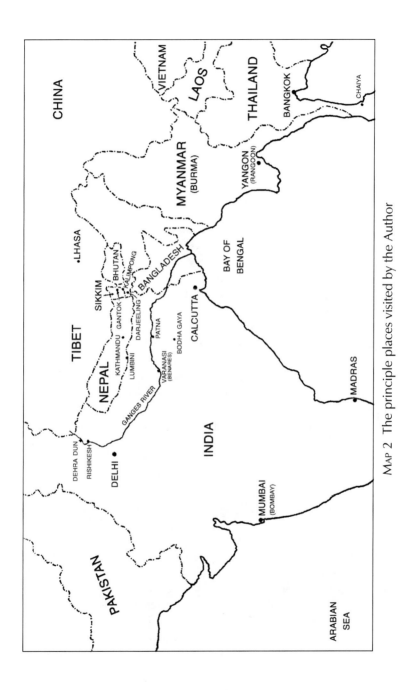

Map 2 The principle places visited by the Author

"But it's important you get there before dawn to make sure you see the sunrise," went on Tenderflower. "That's a sight you will never forget."

We looked at one another. If there's one luxury I look forward to on vacation—and I knew Ed felt the same way—it's the leisure to get up in my own good time. We had not bargained for such an early start. The girls, however, had already decided Tiger Hill was a must and after a meal and a brief tour of the town center, during which we bought souvenirs and fixed a car and driver for the following day, we turned in early, leaving instructions with Tenderflower to give us a shake at 4 a.m. and surprising our driver with the news that he had to be ready to drive us to Tiger Hill at 4:30 next morning. Even Ed and I retired with a pleasant sense of anticipation.

The road was a thin layer of gravel making no pretence of covering the potholes and boulders which enlivened the journey. It wound round the more precipitous inclines as it stretched upwards into the hills and we arrived at the flat open area of Tiger Hill while the sky was still a rich navy blue speckled with bright stars. We had taken the precaution of equipping ourselves with woolen hats which completely enveloped our heads, the eyes just visible through a narrow slit, and we were glad of the warm clothing we'd brought along.

We stomped about and banged our feet and thumped our fists together as the sky gradually paled on the eastern horizon. For a time we wished we were back in the warmth of our beds at the Windermere. Slowly the dim shapes of the skyline came into view and then as if it happened suddenly we saw the majestic snow-capped peak of Everest and, to our right in the distance, Kanchenjunga, tall, magnificent and mysterious.

We had shivered and flung our arms about for a full half-hour when the first ray of sunlight touched the tips of the mountains with an unearthly pink glow. The impact of the moment was mesmerizing and breathtaking. As the raw sun climbed over the distant peaks its horizontal beams flooded the entire panorama with cold light—pink, then orange, then flame red, the deep Himalayan folds throwing rich blue and purple shadows over the roof of the world as far as we could see.

From our vantage point we gazed in awe over hundreds of square miles of the vast mountain range. The girls gasped in amazement at the sheer visual beauty of the scene: we all did. I don't think there was a superlative we didn't use in our astonishment and wonder. We had stopped stamping the ground. We had forgotten how cold we were. We simply stood in rapture as the vivid colors spread and illumined the land. The unforgettable minutes of that daybreak on Tiger Hill were a spiritual experience.

And then it was all over, as suddenly as it had begun. The sun, a huge red globe, moved up in the heavens and where moments ago every crag and indentation had been sharply etched for miles by the penetrating dawn light, now a white haze of damp mist crept up to blot out the view.

The magic evaporated. In minutes even Mount Everest, the world's most daunting summit, was hidden under a blanket of white clouds and we came back to earth, blinked our eyes and snapped out of the trance that had held us.

The silence was broken by our driver "Ready?" he said laconically, with the air of someone who has seen it all before.

"Ready," I agreed, as we all clambered back into our seats, remembering once again that our fingers and toes felt ready to drop off with cold.

I don't think anybody spoke during the ride back to town. If they did I don't recall what they said. But Tenderflower had been right: we all carried back with us a memory we shall keep for the rest of our lives.

❁

It was Jean's idea to call on Sherpa Tenzing at his home in Darjeeling. Having seen Everest for the first time and in such remarkable and memorable circumstances she felt we should complete the experience by meeting someone who had scaled its forbidding walls, and who better than the man who was Sir Edmund Hillary's companion when the first historical conquest of the summit was achieved?

The Tenzing home was among the British-style villas in a good-class part of town and we saw his name on a plate attached to the fence surrounding his front garden. After we had made our introductions the famous mountaineer led us to his study in the front part of the house. Considering we were total strangers who had appeared on his doorstep unannounced and unexpected he gave us a most cordial welcome.

We were fascinated with the mementos he showed us of his achievement, the letters and photographs which he kept as permanent reminders of that day in 1953 when news broke that the world's highest peak had been beaten.

A tough, solidly-built Nepalese, Sherpa Tenzing told me he was a follower of Tibetan Buddhism and that his faith had been a spiritual stimulation during the ordeals he and Hillary faced on their momentous climb.

Back at the hotel we discussed where to go next. I had heard the Tibetan lamas were holding their annual festival at Gantok in Sikkim, which is an Indian protectorate bordering Tibet and some 40 to 50 miles from Darjeeling. It would probably afford me the opportunity to gather knowledge of Tibetan Buddhism from some of its most dedicated adherents and I talked my companions into making the journey with me.

Unfortunately, we were unaware of the restrictions placed on travel into the area by the Indian authorities because of the conflicts which were just at the time beginning with Red China. We went to the Indian District Office, a single-storey wooden structure manned by uniformed civil servants, to acquire the necessary permits and found ourselves face to face with a tall, dour official, an unsmiling man with a thin moustache who, we felt quite certain, would turn down our requests out of hand. We were right.

"I very much regret," he said in an officious tone, "it will be quite impossible to obtain permission to travel into Sikkim." He sounded exactly like an officially worded letter from the Minister of the Interior himself.

"But we'll only be there a short time," I protested. "Just long enough to take a look at the scenery and watch the religious festival."

"I'm sorry, it will be quite impossible," he repeated. "You should have applied months ago when you were in Bangkok. It's no use coming to me now. I don't make the rules, you know."

We began to move towards the door while the liverish Indian returned his attention to the papers on his desk. But although he may not have been responsible for imposing the restrictions it appeared he had the power to relax them for suddenly he looked up and called us back, a smile flickering round his mouth for the first time.

"Although it is highly irregular," he began, as though dictating a memo for his chief to sign, "I will issue the documents permitting you to enter the Protectorate for a short stay but only on account of your obvious respectability."

We were dumbfounded. The tables had turned with such rapidity and on such unlikely grounds as our appearance that we didn't know what to say. The humour of the situation was rich: there we were four intelligence agents of a foreign power attempting to enter a restricted zone which was a potential political flashpoint—admittedly we were off duty and genuinely enjoying a vacational jaunt—and we were being allowed to do so on the evidence of our obvious respectability!

We took our permits, complimented the official on his generosity and obvious wisdom, and hurried away before he had a chance to change his mind.

With our permits, our hired car and our respectability we took leave of the friendly Tenderflowers at the Windermere Hotel and moved off in the direction of Gantok through treacherous mountain passes and more beautiful scenery.

The road was rough and progress slow. When dusk fell we had reached Kalimpong, a small township in the hills near the Sikkim border, and decided to put up for the night. It took only a short time to discover there was no hotel in the place but the natives told us we could find rooms at an orphanage school run by a group of British missionary women. We inquired at the orphanage, a collection of small buildings, and the ladies admitted us cheerfully.

They assigned us separate rooms named after the virtues: I was shown into Peace, while my friends were allocated Hope, Charity and Love. The headmistress told us that when we had settled in we would be welcome to join her and her colleagues at dinner. We washed, changed into lighter clothes and went along to the dining room where the women, about ten of them, were waiting for us.

The room was sparsely furnished, the walls lined with religious prints, and in the center a long table was laid ready for the evening meal. After we had introduced ourselves to the company we all sat down, the headmistress, a prim, graying woman, taking the head of the table with myself on her right.

The questions flowed at once: "Where are you going?" "Where have you been?" The women, all of them more than a little austere in their clothes and their speech, nevertheless were eager to know everything about their guests and about the places we had been and the people we'd met and maintained a lively and vivacious conversation on a variety of subjects

They were charm itself. For all their unusual setting in the heart of the Himalayas and their challenging and devoted vocation as teachers and "mothers" to a hundred or more local children they were vital and interesting people.

When the meal arrived the headmistress served herself first and passed the tray of food to me. I gave myself a generous portion and passed the tray on to Betty, who in turn handed it on to Jean and then to Ed, who passed it on round the table. We had worked up healthy appetites during our journey and were ready for the sizable helpings we allotted ourselves.

But as the tray progressed on its way we realized that the food on it was intended for everyone present, that there was no more where that came from. We were horrified, when the tray reached about three-quarters of the way round, to notice that the missionary women were taking a pea apiece and cutting a slice of carrot into three or four tiny morsels so they could each participate in what food was left.

Our embarrassment was assuaged by the graciousness of our hostess, but in the end they agreed to let us redistribute the portions we had taken on a "fair shares for all" basis which made us all feel a lot better.

Next morning, after a somewhat restrained approach to breakfast, we took off along the road to Gantok feeling refreshed and rested. We passed caravans of yaks coming in the opposite direction bringing their wares into India for the markets. There were prayer flags, like long white streamers, flying throughout the countryside and Tibetan peasants were trotting along the road on their way to the festival, spinning their prayer wheels.

"What on earth are they doing?" asked Jean. I told her the prayer wheel was a kind of instant holiness gadget regarded by many followers of the faith as an integral part of worship. A few spins of the wheel would win the spinner a hundred thousand points of holy merit. The wheel itself is usually made of copper embossed with prayers and religious symbols; the cylindrically shaped wheel is attached to a wooden handle with a short chain and weight on the end to make the wheel spin freely.

No doubt Buddha would have no more approved this type of mechanical cleansing operation for the soul any more than he would the esoteric ritual of the lamas' festivities or the Tantric practices about which I was to learn so much in the days that followed.

Gantok was bustling with excitement. Large crowds were gathered around the monastery area where the festival was to take place. Men and women were dressed up in colorful clothing, beautiful beads and fur-capped hats. Some of the peasants wore magnificently colored blanket coats, fur-collared and with wide bands of yellow, orange and green. Their feet were protected from the cold and the rough terrain by high felt boots studded with pink and turquoise stones.

The ceremony started with the trumpeting sound of the long brass mountain horns at the doors of the temple. The sonorous moan echoed through the hills and heralded the start of a weird sequence of dances by lamas dressed in an assortment of colorful costumes representing the various devils, demons and gods which they wished to appease or to whom their ritualistic religion required them to pay homage. The dancing, supposedly depicting a philosophical symbolization of life forces interacting, went on for hours and we found the whole noisy and colorful scene fascinating.

I thought if I could single out one of the lamas who was not participating actively in the demonstration I might be able to persuade him to tell me something of the fundamental differences between the varieties of Buddhism, those variants practiced in the neighborhood we were at present visiting and those of other schools in Burma, Thailand, Ceylon, Cambodia, Vietnam and Laos.

I realized all too well there was likely to be a language problem and looked about, perhaps a little hopelessly, for a holyman who looked as if he might speak English. It was worth a try and, having come so far, I didn't fancy returning home, with only the memory of the visual spectacle as evidence of my visit.

Luck was on my side for finally I did notice in the crowd a lama whose facial features looked European although he wore a striking violet red robe and sandals and his head was clean-shaven. Betty, Jean and Ed moved off to mingle with the throng while I approached my "find" and asked straight out if he spoke English.

"I am French, but I have a little English," he answered. He had a high voice and a strong French accent. We shook hands and I explained my mission as simply as I could.

"Please go ahead and put your questions," he said agreeably, "I will answer to the best of my ability."

For more than an hour we stood in the town square exchanging question and answer while all around us the excitement and fever of the festival raged in a riot of discordant noise and color. The situation was bizarre, perhaps, but I was collecting valuable material—and direct from the horse's mouth.

It couldn't have been better. My informant was knowledgeable, lucid and cooperative even though I knew he might well have preferred to take part in the day's activities rather than stand talking on the sidelines to an inquisitive stranger.

When our conversation came to an end I had learned much about the workings of the Tibetan Buddhist's mind, learned also that there was still a great deal I had to witness at first hand if I was to make my understanding of Eastern religions anything like complete.

When I thanked my informant for his helpfulness and exchanged names I got the shock of my life: "he" turned out to be a woman. Abashed, I mumbled my embarrassed apologies for not latching on to the fact sooner, though I must say in my own defence there was good reason for the mistake. Her brightly colored robes had fooled me, for in my experience only the monks were dressed in garments of saffron or other colors: nuns always wore white.

She was amused at my confusion. I did not exactly ask my mademoiselle lama what a nice girl like her was doing in a place like this: in the first place it would have seemed disrespectful and in any case I didn't have to.

She told me she had undertaken the study of Buddhism only a short time before and planned to spend the next few years in Sikkim pursuing meditative practices in her search for enlightenment and truth. I have often wondered about her since. She told me nothing of her background or of her reasons for withdrawing from the world in that remote and lonely corner of the Himalayas.

The French nun, both in the information she imparted and in the advice she gave me for pursuing further research while I was in Gantok, proved instrumental in helping to crystallize for me the dominant features of Tibetan mysticism. She directed me to a meditation center where I could see for myself the processes by which its students attained mental liberation.

I found that the whole Tibetan tradition is rich in symbolism and ritual; the dances I had witnessed were an example of this. The cornerstone of their symbolization is perhaps the use of *mantra* or the repetition of a single word over and over again which to some extent has the effect of quieting the mind.

The commonest word in use in this mantra process is *om*—I think it is more a soporific sound than an actual word—and I heard the rhythmic murmurings of om...om...om repeated in continuous low tones by the monks and their disciples in all the temples I visited at Gantok.

Om has a significant place in Tibetan religious lore: it is of prime importance to the understanding of the lamas' symbolic teaching. It is integrally associated with liberation either as a means to it or as a symbol of its attainment.

Om to one person can be a symbol of the divine universe, to another infinite power. To one individual om may mean infinity, to another it may symbolize an infinite being or life eternal. The mesmeric hum of om...om...om means peace and a quiet mind in the heights of meditation. It means boundless knowledge, omnipresent light, universal law, omnipotent consciousness, all pervading divinity, all-encompassing love, cosmic rhythm, ever present creativeness and so on.

Mantra, then, the use of a repeated word to awaken deep and copious meditation, is the symbolization in aural terms; it is the holy sound transmitted from the teacher to the disciple during the ritual of initiation and in the course of spiritual discipline. As my informative French nun put it, the inner oscillation set up by this sacred sound and its associations in the consciousness of the disciple opens his mind to experience higher states.

But what of the visual and tangible forms of symbolism in Tibetan Buddhism? The lotus flower is, of course, the traditional Buddhist symbol of spiritual unfoldment; it is in evidence wherever

Buddhists practise Buddhism. In Gantok I found the visual aspect went a great deal further. Almost anything could be used as a symbol, including parts of the body.

I watched a lama practicing *mudra*, a curious and intricate gesturing of the hands which, taken in conjunction with the incessant om…om of mantra and other ritualistic acts, expresses and emphasizes the inner attitude. I was impressed with the amount of talking, acting and gesturing which some of the holymen found a necessary part of their devotions.

Another visual symbol for worship which I learned about at a monastery in Gantok is the *vajra*. It takes the form of a scepter, the embodiment of supreme sovereign power, and has as its principal symbolic point of interest a diamond. It helps the student, I was told, to find the jewel, or *mani*, in his own mind—in other words his highest mental value.

There is an interesting parallel between the vajra and the principle of worship in the Tantric tradition, in which a weakness is turned into a source of strength. My French lady lama told me the story of a king who was being influenced by a yogi to follow the path of the Buddha. The king protested that he could not possibly wear the garb of an ascetic when his high position demanded that he clothe himself in fine garments and adorn himself with exquisite jewelry.

The yogi, realizing the importance the king placed on his jewels, turned the situation to advantage by instructing the royal novice to concentrate his mind on the gems of his bracelet. The king found this acceptable and, following the yogi's advice, he meditated thus until his mind attained the purity of a flawless jewel.

The story was told to me to illustrate the Tantric beliefs but I found overtones of vajra in it also. It has a denouement. The king, now enlightened, told his subjects: "It is not my riches that make me a king, but what I have attained spiritually through my own efforts. My inner peace is my kingdom."

I discussed the Tantric practices briefly both with the French nun and with lamas at the Gantok meditation center; they embody a branch of Buddhism which builds its symbolism upon the polarity of the male and female. In origin it is Tibetan, though a slightly different variant, which I was to find out more about later, is practiced widely in Hindu circles in India.

The Tantras brought religious experience from the abstract plane of speculation down to earth, not, however, with the intention of secularizing it, but to realize it, to make it an active religious force. A very important aspect of Tibetan mysticism and meditation are the symbolization of space, colors, elements, gestures and the spiritual qualities. An important object of their worship, apart from Buddha himself, is *Tara*, the female embodiment of wisdom. She plays a significant role in the religious life of Tibet because of her special qualities representing loving devotion. Tara can be compared to a Madonna uniting in herself all human and divine traits, a kind of mother figure. There is also much meditation on images very similar to some of the more orthodox Christian practices, and rituals employed in, for example, Catholicism.

There is one other aspect of Tibetan meditation to which I have so far not alluded but it has its place in any survey of the scene and while I saw no sign of it at Gantok one of the lamas at the monastery mentioned it to me.

In essence it is believed that there are psychic centers of the body, each with its psychological counterpart. By this is meant that various parts of the person function physiologically in conjunction with, and representative of, certain psychological activity. I was told—and found the idea rather hard to accept—that functions of the arms, fingers, legs, abdomen and even the genitals reflect an activity of the psyche.

My assessment of the religious practices of the Tibetan lamas could not be as penetrating as I would have wished but to me this journey was useful in that it gave me an insight into one more of the many faces of Eastern meditative philosophy. My mini-investigation in Sikkim provided further valuable food for thought in my pursuit of a quiet mind and I found that although I could not accept everything I saw and heard as valid religious sense, neither could I reject it.

I felt certain, however, that my old friend Krishnamurti would not tolerate much that I had encountered at Gantok. Some time later I came across a book Mary Lutyens had written from his sayings and it proved me right. "There are systems of meditation," said Krishnamurti, "which give you a word and tell you that if you go on repeating it you will have some extraordinary transcendental experience. This is sheer nonsense. It is a form of self-hypnosis."

He even went further. "By repeating Amen or om or Coca-Cola indefinitely you obviously have a certain experience because by repetition the mind becomes quiet—meditation is not following any system; it is not constant repetition and imitation. It is one of the favorite gambits of some teachers of meditation to insist on their pupils learning concentration, that is, fixing the mind on one thought and driving out all other thoughts. This is a most stupid, ugly thing, which any schoolboy can do because he is forced to."

Such scornful words amply illustrate Krishnamurti's views on the Tibetan lamas' mantra and my own understanding of his teaching leads me to agree. He has told me that all stimulation inevitably brings about dependence and this in turn prevents us from seeing clearly and freely. Discipline does not quiet the mind, it merely makes it dull. Control produces conflict.

Among the dignitaries who attended the festival ceremony was the then Maharaja of Sikkim. He had had a tent set up for entertaining the lamas and as there were only a few foreigners present he invited me to join him for a meal and to bring my friends along too. An excellent conversationalist and an intelligent person, he expressed grave concern for the plight of the Tibetan people under the oppression of Communist China. His fears, of course, were justified for as far as one can tell from what little news has reached the outside world the religion and traditions by which the Tibetans set such store have been completely suppressed.

Betty, Jean, Ed and I had to get a move on if we were to catch the plane back to Bangkok from Darjeeling the next day. We left with some regrets, for the town was still agog with movement, strange sounds and fascinating sights. I have often longed to return, but Sikkim is completely sealed off to foreigners and likely to remain so for a very long time.

10

Nepal, Land of Gods—and Beatniks

ONE of the "bonus" pleasures of my investigation into the mysteries of Eastern cultures in my quest for the true meaning of a quiet mind was the opportunity for sightseeing it afforded and the chances it gave me to observe the indigenous habits of the people whose countries I visited.

I hope I have been able to convey something of these incidental delights in my account of the various journeys I undertook. A local custom I encountered in Bombay, however, was one I would prefer to have missed.

I had spent a hot and grueling day interviewing a number of religious leaders, yogis and *gurus* and now wished to find a cool spot where I could rest my legs and reflect over what I had seen and heard.

The only place I knew which would fit the bill with its air-conditioned splendor and general atmosphere of comfort and relaxation was the bar at the Taj Mahal Hotel. Hot and weary, I entered the ornate portals of the famous hotel, walked into the bar and ordered a Coca Cola from the waiter; then I sat down with a sigh of utter relief in the nearest chair.

"Can I see your license, sir?" said the waiter.

"License?" I said. "License for what?"

The waiter explained that Bombay was a "dry" state and anyone who wished to buy a drink in the area needed a license.

"But that's ridiculous," I protested. "All I want is a Coke, nothing alcoholic."

"I'm sorry, sir," he replied. "But you will have to leave the bar unless you can produce a license. One is not allowed to stay here without a license."

There was obviously nothing for it but to leave, but before I did so the bartender explained that if I returned later in the evening I could meet a government official who would be there to issue licenses. I ambled out into the sun again, a little fresher for my brief cooling whiff of the bar's air conditioning system, but otherwise rather hot under the collar and muttering angrily that I'd only wanted a Coke after all and I couldn't understand why I should be required to show a permit before I could enter a bar. My complaints got me nowhere, however.

There was one more person I wished to see that day and I hailed a taxi and gave the driver directions to take me to a certain suburban area of Bombay. I had heard of a Hindu sage, a former medical doctor, who was desperately trying to gather around him a following for his particular brand of Hindu teaching. I had heard he was having something of a struggle to win adherents for his methods and when I met him I quickly understood why.

At his retreat were a number of students, including a few Thai Buddhist monks. They were listening intently to the sage, who cut a striking figure in his white muslin robes and long flowing white beard, but they were finding his words heavy going. Not only was he unnecessarily verbose in expression but his message seemed to depend on a very high level of intellectual projection. In short, he was not coming across at all well.

His recipe for the achievement of nirvana or the quiet mind seemed to turn upside down all I had learned and practiced: instead of clearing the mind of distracting impedimenta he taught an Indian *vedantic* system in which the student is made to concentrate on a theme to the exclusion of all else.

While focussing his attention on a theme such as "God the holy, God the holy and mighty, holy and immortal, be gracious unto us! Blessed be thou, O Lord," or "What is mind? Only a bundle of thoughts; stop thinking and show me then where is the mind," the mind is supposed to become a power with far-reaching range. Up to a point this is similar to the use of mantra but with the difference that the mind is kept working and busy.

The sage mentioned a variety of holy themes on which it was

beneficial to concentrate: the *Gita* or Hindu bible, the *Dhamma* or Buddhist bible, and the Christian Bible were appropriate subjects. Leading thinkers including Sri Aurobindo, Ramana Maharishi and Sankaracharya could be useful subjects also. What puzzled me was how all this mental activity could possibly lead to a quiet mind.

I felt this yogi's teaching was not for me. His Hindu and Brahmin intellectualism went well above my head and, with as much courtesy as I could muster after a hard day in the sun, I turned down his invitation to become a recruit to his peculiar line of thinking.

Now, I thought, I will return to the Taj Mahal, meet the civil servant who dishes out the drink licenses, and really take the weight off my feet while enjoying a well-earned Coke in the plush bar.

The official was there as promised, elaborately decked out in uniform with braid and medals, and complete with briefcase stuffed with forms, documents and rubber stamps for the issuing of liquor licenses. He explained that if I was a bona fide tourist he could issue a temporary license for immediate use. If, on the other hand, I was a resident of India I would have to get a certificate from a registered medical practitioner declaring that I was an alcoholic, in which case a resident's license would be issued.

Once again I tried to explain that I only wanted a soft drink and to take advantage of the comfortable air-conditioned surroundings of the bar. He was sorry, but a license was absolutely necessary. In the end I filled out a long form, paid for tax stamps and became the holder of a Bombay drink permit. Immediately I ordered my Coke.

While all this was going on I was aware of two non-teetotal residents standing at the bar with whiskies and sodas in their hands and paying careful attention to everything that passed between the government official and myself. As soon as the absurd proceedings were over they pounced. They had used up their allotted quota of liquor coupons for the month and, as I was evidently not a drinker, begged me to let them have my unused coupons in exchange for as much Coca Cola as I could drink free of charge on them. I happily obliged.

❋

I had made several trips to India with the intention of venturing into Nepal to see the birthplace of Gotama Buddha and study further whatever evidence I could find of the Tantrism practiced by Buddhists in the thousands of monasteries in northern India and Tibet.

On previous occasions there had always been something to prevent this ambition being realized. This time all systems were go. My visa was in order, weather conditions were right and there was an available flight at the time when I wanted it. The air trip from Delhi into the vale of Kathmandu was a rewarding one. The day was clear, the sun was bright in the sky and the scene from the aircraft windows was magnificent.

All the rugged grandeur of the Himalayan foothills stretched out for miles in every direction revealing the great natural beauty of the area in all its splendor. When I caught my first glimpse of Kathmandu, the once forbidden city, in the distance I felt a thrill of anticipation.

The plane dropped down on Kathmandu airport around mid morning. My first impression on leaving the airport and walking in the streets was of the complete lack of organization or pattern about the layout of the buildings and the charming disorder of the people themselves.

There was a quaint mingling of old and new, culture and poverty, the secular and the religious which lent the ancient city an immense charm. There were carvings of gods everywhere, brightly colored. Animals wandered about listlessly among the open-air stalls.

It was a scene of contrasts. In the market place, medieval brick dwellings rubbed shoulders with Buddhist temples and modern office blocks of attractive architectural merit. Some of the people wore modern Western-style clothes while some of the women were clad in traditional long skirts of black with red-banded hems. Small children ran about wearing nothing. I noticed that the Nepalese, an Indian-Mongolian mixture, are a strikingly handsome race with wide and lustrous dark eyes.

Another contrast and one I was glad of was the Annapurna Hotel where I had reserved a room. With its deep-piled carpets and modern appurtenances it was an oasis of order and comfort in this strange city, and when I had closed the door in my room, which was fully equipped with modern fittings including air-conditioning which doubled as central heating when the nights got cold, I found it hard to believe

I was so far from civilization as I knew it. If Kathmandu was out of this world the Annapurna Hotel was well and truly in it.

With the hotel as my base I set out on an initial sortie of the neighborhood to orientate myself and size up the situation. For the purpose I hired a bicycle rickshaw and the driver sped me away on a rapid but fascinating tour of the main tourist highspots. Kathmandu is a photographer's dream world.

First stop was the Hanuman Dhoka, ancient ruined palace of the kings with the stone figure of the monkey god Hanuman squatting at the gates. There was a prolifery of multistoried pagodas, temples and shrines, their beams intricately carved with gods and human figures in the act of copulation in a somewhat breathtaking variety of attitudes. I have read that the scenes are supposed to shock the virgin Goddess of Lightning and as a result she spares the buildings. Personally I doubt if such scenes shock anyone in the Nepal region any more, there are so many of them.

There were more temples than houses, more gods than citizens— at least that was the impression Kathmandu made upon me that day. And subsequent investigation bore out the truth of this. In no other country is the deity more in evidence in the streets, on the buildings, everywhere; nor in a greater multiplicity of forms. Their worship was the most common activity, furthermore, and I saw more people engaged in some kind of religious devotion than doing productive work.

My conversations with the inhabitants confirmed that religion is the center of life for Kathmandu's population. No other activity claims so much attention for they regard everything they do as a form of worship and every human action merely as a manifestation of the divine. Eating, working, birth, sexual union, death are the physical and material manifestations of the divine process and their holy import always transcended their functional value.

This, then, was the ultra religious environment in which this community went about their daily lives and in which my search now led me. Not far away at Lumbini near the Indian border was the birthplace of Buddha himself. I wondered what the revered founder of the faith of millions would have to say about the extents to which some of his worshippers went in their homage.

I have already referred in passing to the Tantric traditions in

Buddhism but my knowledge of this limb of the religion was scanty, even after my meeting with the French nun in Sikkim and my talks with holymen in the places of worship I visited at Gantok. What knowledge I had was based on hearsay and I must record that I felt most of it to be ill-founded and inaccurate. In Kathmandu I had an excellent chance to find out the truth and I intended to leave no avenue unexplored in my efforts to get at the facts.

I should reemphasize the point, however, that I find it difficult to accept the Tantric customs as a true expression of Buddhism, despite their widespread practice. The teachings of Buddha, who was himself born a Hindu, created a more civilized form of Hinduism just as the gospel of Jesus Christ civilized the Jehovan creed. But as Christ's teaching to "love thy neighbor" was perverted to justify the Inquisition, so the Buddha's teaching degenerated to Lamaism and Tantric Buddhism with its emphasis on ritualistic sexual activities. The erotic carvings I saw in Nepal have their origins in Tantrism which in turn was a deviation from Buddhist moral temperance.

Sex in Nepal, incidentally, is taken very much for granted. There is a complete absence of prostitution and pornography is unknown in the bookshops. The Nepalese themselves are said to be free from impotence, frigidity, sexual frustration and guilt complexes and no doubt there are very few psychiatric couches there as a result of Hinduism's tolerant approach to sex and Tantric Buddhism's sexuality. Just how vital a part sex played in the religion of the area and the importance attached to its symbolism was to be unfolded to me in the following days.

My most informative source was a high Tibetan monk and distinguished exponent who was held in considerable esteem throughout the land. An octogenarian, his years detracted nothing from his mental adroitness and his readiness to discuss the various aspects of the religious life of the community with a stranger. In addition, I was glad to find he spoke excellent English. With this learned old scholar I was able to dig fairly deeply and in some detail into the facets of Tibetan religious practice and its contrasts with Hinduism. Much of what he told me made a good deal of sense but there was, to a man with my origins and background, a lot that was not so acceptable.

The whole question, it seemed to me (for I am interpreting what the old man told me), hinged on the sexuality of the male and female as the basic creative force. From this the act of sexual intercourse itself, the union of two bodies, emerged as the most potent physical incentive or urge known to mankind. The purpose of the Tantric practices was to harness this polarity or sexual attraction and to equate the physical performance with a spiritual enlightenment.

The link between the sex act and its spiritual impact on the mind was the moment of orgasm which, while only lasting seconds in most cases, raised the participants to a transcendental state in which spiritual enlightenment could be achieved. If the subjects were in meditation at this crucial moment, the greater was the effect upon the spirit and the nearer one came to that elusive state in which the mind was quiet.

It is common knowledge in the Himalayas as anywhere else that sex, the attraction of man for woman and girl for boy, and the delights of sexual experience, can become obsessive. As such it can create an impediment to the normal full functioning of an individual in whom it is allowed to monopolize his thoughts. This applies as much to a holyman who has taken vows of chastity as to anyone else. The Tantric belief is that the orgasm and the ritual of going through a sexual experience in properly conducted circumstances, usually in the sacred surroundings of a temple or monastery, will liberate the mind from sexual domination.

In other words it is thought possible to overcome sexual obsession by practicing sex, and thus leave the mind clear for more important activity.

This draining of the libido, however temporary the resultant state, seems to be an important aspect of the Tantric doctrine though probably not its overriding purpose. My high lama informant emphasized more than once that the use of sexual intercourse or other forms of sexual self-satisfaction during the course of a monk's devotions was never regarded frivolously as an entertainment or an enjoyment.

Far from it. Sex, after all, was the most basic of functions, the most down-to-earth of man's natural impulses, and if by the use of sex it was possible to identify oneself closely with nature then it was a means to achieve, or try to achieve, self-knowledge. It is natural in the human makeup to have inhibitions as well as obsessions with regard to sex, but here again the regular, controlled indulgence of it will overcome those inhibitions and lead gradually to awareness.

But I wondered if there was not something even more complex

and deep-rooted about the symbolization of sexual union in Tantric teachings. The lama agreed there was. The operative word, he said, was union. Union of the male and female bodies for creative purposes was one thing, but the use of union in the Tantric religion meant much more; it was the union of the male and female characteristics, personal and spiritual qualities which lead to self-awareness, the ability to recognize within oneself those elements which were normally associated with the other partner. The ability, in the case of the male, to recognize in himself qualities of tenderness and lovingness, and in the case of the female, the ability to see in her constitution an element of aggressiveness or responsibility or forcefulness, personality characteristics normally associated with the male.

This aspect highlights one of the contrasts between the Tibetan and Hindu presentations of the Tantric doctrine. In Tibetan symbolization such as the carvings on temple walls in Kathmandu the male partner featured in the scenes of copulation is always shown as the active and dominant figure while the female plays a passive role. In Hindu tradition the positions are reversed so that the female takes on the more active role normally associated with the male. This is not capriciousness; it is a symbolization of true union.

What I found rather hard to accept, looking at these bizarre practices from the point of view of a fairly typical Westerner, was the apparent absence of a simple thing called love. To most of my friends and acquaintances (and I hope most of my readers) love usually plays at least a moderately important part in the sex act. We have a phrase, lovemaking, which we often prefer to the bald and clinical sounding expression "sexual intercourse." Love exists in Nepal as it does elsewhere and during my stay I met several families as happy and loving as those in my own home town. But in the religious application of sex, *love* was absent, it was the sex drive itself, the buildup, the ejaculation, the transcendental moment of orgasm, the sense of spiritual and physical release with its attendant purging and clarifying of the mind which were the quintessence and substance of the teaching.

I had heard that Tantrism permitted its devotees to seek sexual union within the family circle and that religious sexual intercourse with one's sister or mother was an acceptable means of achieving self-knowledge. Even if this is untrue, and the lama refuted the suggestion when I put it to him, it does illustrate the kind of detached approach to sexual activity displayed by the Tantric mind.

I have not told the full story. There is more to Tantrism than I was able to find out in my first study of the subject among the temples of Nepal. Its followers are devout and upright men and women and although its customs ring strange in our ears and would perhaps offend the sensibilities of even the most broad-minded among Western Sunday churchgoers its disciples, I was convinced, were genuine in their search for self-knowledge and the quiet mind.

For myself, I felt there was little I could gain by joining in their practices. I felt very much out of tune with their thinking and came away with some extra knowledge, for which I have to thank the lama in particular, but no nearer my goal.

I wondered if the beatniks and hippies, who at that time were congregating in Kathmandu, achieved what they were looking for. They were weird-looking youngsters, bedraggled and forlorn, and were to be seen all around the city. At my hotel another visitor was a Pakistani businessman who was in Nepal for the purpose of going on a tiger hunt. One day we went into a coffee shop where the beatniks and hippies gathered to smoke hashish which is sold without restriction there. We drank some soft drinks and had a bowl of stewed yak as we watched the collection of motley youths murmuring together in huddles, sometimes singing and by all appearances happily whiling away their time and doing no harm to anyone. They were offbeat, but for the most part those we talked to were intelligent, adventurous youngsters with more hair than money out to see the world.

I think I met one man in Kathmandu who had achieved all he required out of life: Boris Lissanevitch, owner and manager of the Royal Hotel. A White Russian, he told me he had come to the kingdom of Nepal at the time of the Russian Revolution and liked the "land of the temples" so much he stayed.

His story was a fascinating one. With his flair for catering he had come to the notice of the Nepalese royal family who in the course of time made him their official caterer. When his appointment lapsed he went into business on his own and acquired one of the ancient Rana palaces which he turned into a hotel on the grand scale. The Ranas were the autocratic dynasty of Prime Ministers who ruled by hereditary right until their regime was overthrown in the 1950s and the monarchy restored to power.

Today people visit Boris from all parts of the world and gaze in admiration and wonder upon the lavish trappings of his aptly named Royal Hotel, with its gilt ornaments, enormous chandeliers and rich, plush drapes. The walls are decorated with magnificent oil paintings of the Ranas in uniforms of red with gold braid, medals and jeweled swords, and on their heads the fantastic Rana helmets inlaid with precious stones and decked with birds of Paradise feathers.

I chatted with Boris on a number of occasions in his "Yak and Yeti" bar with its copper chimneyed open fire and in surroundings of warmth and luxury. Although I was staying at the more sophisticated Annapurna with its accent on modern comforts I found myself taking most of my meals at the exotic Royal. I could not help reflecting that here at least was a man who had found satisfaction in life.

It was with a sad heart that I left Nepal after that first visit, for its easygoing casual life and charm certainly made one question the merits of returning to the metropolitan bustle and action of Bangkok.

To go to Kathmandu is to step back in time; there's an enchantment about it which can be found in no other place. When I caught my plane it was to fly once again into the twentieth century. Which, of course, was where I belonged.

On my next trip to Kathmandu, not long after, I took my wife with me. We had met during a visit I'd made to London and after something of a whirlwind romance I had married her and carried her off to Thailand. I wanted to show her, among many other wonderful features of this remarkable landscape, the great Bodhnath Stupa temple perched on the summit of a hill on the outskirts of the city. We hired a taxi, the most convenient form of transport in these parts, and it dropped us at a grove at the foot of the hill. The shrine was an impressive spectacle with its large white dome-shaped pagoda base: a solid hemisphere of brick and earth some sixty feet across.

The base supported a gilt rectangular plinth decorated with the all-seeing eyes of Buddha on each of its surfaces, supposedly keeping a watch on all the deeds of the faithful and those of the not-so-faithful, too. Towering above this to a height of 250 feet was the temple's conical gold spire with a pinnacle of copper gilt

We began the long climb up the stairway leading to the temple, overtaking on the way a Tibetan smiling peacefully to himself and piously spinning his prayer wheel, and at last reached the top and approached the central area at the base of the pagoda. We were literally surrounded by temples, monasteries and carved images of every shape and size, with the magnificent Bodhnath Stupa, the world's oldest and most spectacular Buddhist shrine, a glittering center piece under the blue sky.

A Hindu service was taking place on the pavement at the base of the Stupa. A priest was chanting and gesturing around some candles, incense sticks, flowers and other symbolic paraphernalia. A handful of followers were bowing and scraping, chanting and praying. We tried to determine the significance of the service but no one spoke English and we had to draw our own conclusions from the visual impressions and our imaginations.

A monkey leapt over our heads on to the wall surrounding the area. There were monkeys everywhere. They seemed to have found a haven of safety away from the harsh life of the forest.

Suddenly we heard a commotion coming from the far side of the area. We walked in the direction of the noise and came upon a Tibetan temple consisting of a large hall very ornately decorated. Inside, the high lama was seated on a raised platform facing a group of eight monks who were making heavy music from a weird assortment of gongs, drums, horns and stringed instruments and chanting all the while.

A small congregation of pilgrims were in the temple joining in the ceremony and everyone turned to stare at the two foreign intruders. We hand signaled the high lama for permission to take photographs and this pleased the musical company. An outstanding feature of decor in the temple was an enormous prayer wheel near the back wall behind the musicians.

Again we tried to find out what the ceremony was all about but again the language barrier proved insuperable. It appeared to be a routine service paying homage to Buddha with a sermon by the high lama taken from the holy books.

Until 1951 Nepal, occupying a strip of no more than 54,000 square miles along the slopes of the Himalayas bounded by India on one frontier and Tibet on the other, and with a population something less than that of London, was cut off from the world both by its mountains and its despotic Rana rulers. Today all that is changed.

The high Himalaya country, the foothills and the low, swampy Terai famous for its big game, are tourist haunts.

The country is rich in archaeological treasures and the art and architecture of the inhabitants provided the most unusual sightseeing opportunities of any in the world. It is said that the Nepalese architects built the temples and monasteries of Lhasa, the holy city of Tibet. Until the late 1950s the only routes into Nepal, other than by air, were rough, narrow tracks through steep mountain passes. Today a motor road links the valley of Kathmandu with India.

The first tourists came in 1955—ten Americans and two Brazilians on a Thomas Cook tour—and in 1956 the King, once more restored to his throne, was crowned in a lavish and colorful ceremony which was filmed by Cinerama and attended by newsmen from many countries.

11

Tantrism: an On-the-Spot Investigation

I WAS to hear more about the Tantric practices during a visit to Benares a short time later. Benares, the holy city of the Hindus and one of the most ancient cities of the world, is an important center of Buddhism and in addition to many ruins testifying to its religious importance in the past it also boasts between 1,500 and 2,000 modern temples within its boundaries.

Seen from the Ganges the city has an appearance of great beauty and even at closer quarters there is about its cramped streets and its bustling, crowded lanes and quaint buildings a mystery and a charm which to a visitor is a constant fascination.

It was my habit when I visited a center such as this, rich in material for my researches, to walk or ride about the streets at leisure getting the feel of the place and planning my mode of operations. At Benares I was sickened by much that I saw: the filth everywhere, the beggars with their gangrenous injuries, the leprous children some of whom had had their arms or legs broken to arouse the sympathy of tourists and induce them to pour coins into the tiny, dirty outstretched hands.

The Ganges itself, the sacred river, was the color of coffee with milk. Wide-mouthed sewer pipes spewed the town's effluent into it with utter disregard for hygiene while a little further along the bank a primitive laundry was in operation on quite a large scale. Sheets, towels and clothing were being washed in the stinking polluted waters then pounded against the rocks on the river side and spread out in the sun to dry. I saw the burning ghats where devout Hindus are cremated and learned that it is the ambition of all the wealthier Hindus to be taken to Benares when they die so that their ashes can be scattered on the holy river.

Sometimes the cremation is not as efficient as it could be with the result that charred remains and unburned parts of human bodies floating on the river are not an uncommon sight. I even saw the corpse of a small child drifting in the sluggish murk.

I don't believe it's a visitor's right to criticize or deride native customs but when I had observed the hundreds of holy pilgrims bathing in the Ganges at Benares to wash away their sins I mentioned to an acquaintance, a Spanish Catholic priest whom I had met in the city, that I thought they were likely to pick up more than they washed away. He told me a strange thing. Although one would think the river at this point would be alive with harmful bacteria the water was tested regularly by experts and always found to be absolutely pure. It would seem churlish to say I was unconvinced, but I made sure I didn't linger long by the banks of the holy Ganges.

Father Jose, like me, was in Benares to take a look at local religious customs. I got on well with him. He was short, with a round face usually smiling, and his shaven hair had been allowed to grow into a kind of bristling crew cut. He spoke good English and was evidently from a well-to-do family in Barcelona. He wore ordinary Western clothes. One day I told him I wished to pay a visit to Sarnath which is about six miles outside the city limits of Benares and where Buddha preached his first sermons twenty-five centuries ago. We decided to make the pilgrimage together.

Sarnath was in total contrast to the squalor and bustle and unhealthy atmosphere of Benares. The small town was well taken care of, clean and neat; there were lush gardens everywhere, a few shops and houses well kept and smart in appearance, and several temples both Chinese and Tibetan representing the various schools of Buddhism. Main attraction to visitors was a new temple built by the Mahabodhi Society, its walls decorated with somewhat mediocre paintings of Buddhist scenes by a Japanese artist.

We saw ancient relics of the past in the ruins of temples and pagodas ravaged by the passage of time. We visited the museum which had an excellent collection of Buddhist art. I marveled at the devotion of the pilgrims who were paying their respects to their teacher in the temples of Sarnath and at the painstaking artistry that had gone into the effigies we admired at the museum. But I could not help reflecting that Buddha himself would spurn these artificial trappings of religion, as he would the prayer wheels in Sikkim and the elaborate dancing and rituals of worship. They were mere substitutes, unnecessary paraphernalia, whereas his plea had been for direct action by oneself.

As in all religions, the followers deviated from the truth of direct action and created through interpretations their own images, edifices, rituals and symbols to satisfy their egos. The truly enlightened had transcended their egos and hoped others might do likewise. No, I felt sure the Buddha who propounded his truths in this very spot so long ago would certainly not condone the constructions and practices that had evolved from his clear and enlightened teaching.

From the pleasant haven of Sarnath, Father Jose and I decided to go on to Bodh Gaya where the Buddha, as I have described in an earlier chapter, reputedly reached enlightenment by sitting for weeks under a bodhi tree. It meant a six hour journey by train and the experienced Father Jose said it was essential to travel first class. I soon saw why.

We were accompanied by throngs of peasants with their voluminous belongings, including farm animals, who inundated the train and took up positions in every available corner as their accommodation for the journey. Had we not traveled first class and kept the door of our compartment firmly locked we were quite likely to have been swamped by squealing children and their baggage or goats.

At Bodh Gaya we were awed by the tremendous monuments erected to the memory of Buddha. Here again were the numerous temples where monks from the various Buddhist schools of thought lived and offered a welcome to their followers. Each temple had its own peculiar architectural characteristics redolent of the country it represented and always the devotees visiting Bodh Gaya from these countries stuck to their own areas, whether they hailed from Tibet, China, Japan or Thailand. On the banks of the Niranjana River, silhouetted against a range of low hills, stood the main temple with its imposing 170-foot high pyramidal tower leveled off at the top and crowned by a bell-shaped stupa. Inside was a large gilded image of Buddha.

Since there were no hotels in the town we went to the Thai temple and asked if we might put up there for the night. We were received with great hospitality, offered food and drink and invited to stay for as long as we liked. We joined the holymen in a simple meal of curry, chopped rice, vegetables, chicken and fish, washed down with tea, and afterwards we were shown our rooms. There were about thirty rooms available for visiting pilgrims; each furnished with a simple bed, a chair and a sink with running water.

Next morning we set out to see as much as we could of the sacred rites practiced by the monks who dwelt in the area. We found one of the most astonishing sights was at the monument and shrine constructed on the site of the bodhi tree. Here Tibetan faithful were gaining merit by dragging themselves on their bellies over the long concrete path leading to the shrine. It certainly was a most humble way of declaring their devotion but Buddha would surely not have sanctioned such a display of theatricals.

Every night the Tibetans held an orgy of ritual chanting, praying, bowing and scraping and we were careful not to miss it. There were several hundred oil lamps lit up on altars and the entire area of the monument was illuminated with an orange glow. After several hours of very active ceremony, weird, colorful and noisy against the black night sky, the Tibetan participants brought the elaborate proceedings to an impressive close by throwing offerings of rice to the Buddha all over the altars and the oil lamps, many of which by this time had burned themselves out.

This was the signal for the crowds of onlookers to pounce and help themselves to as much rice as they could get their hands on. Bodh Gaya lies in the heart of the famine area of India where, at the time of my visit, thousands had recently died of starvation. Every night hundreds of hungry natives, adults and children, flocked to the Tibetan ceremony and waited for this moment. When it came there was a crazy rush and they fell on their knees and scraped up every grain of rice they could find to cram into their empty stomachs.

Father Jose knew that I wished to gather further data on the Tantric customs and beliefs and as there was little to be learned at Bodh Gaya that I did not know already he promised to introduce me to a Tibetan lama at the University of Benares who was an authority on the subject. We boarded the train again, locked ourselves in, and returned to Benares with a fund of memories to ponder over.

I was perhaps a bit disheartened to think that so many who live by the Buddhist faith seemed, if I understood his teachings at all, to miss the point. His message, surely, was that the truth lies within the self, that the aim of those who live by his word must be genuine enlightenment by *transcending* all the gaudy nonsense of ritual and sophisticated forms of worship.

❀

I went to meet the lama at Benares with mixed feelings. He was a scholarly figure, younger than I expected, and he made a thorough study of the Tantric faith with its strange and weird practices of worship and ways of ascending to enlightenment. But I wondered if he was also a protagonist of them and a believer in their value. Somehow I never got around to putting that question to him for he spoke so rapidly, and with such donnish authority, that I felt it would be unreasonable to ask point-blank whether he saw positive qualities in what he was describing or merely found it an absorbing subject from the point of view of a student of religion. He gave me a good deal of his time and went out of his way to help: I couldn't bring myself to challenge him on his own attitude.

Personally, I couldn't help feeling that, as in so many of the modern day interpretations of the wisdom of enlightened religious leaders, the Tantric activities originated out of convenience rather than a proper understanding of Buddha's plea for direct experience.

Tantrism, however, turned out to be a complex and abstruse religion whose intricacies, when I had got to the root of them, defied anything more than the most academic attention in my researches. The worship of phallic symbols and idols representing the male and female generative organs was an outward manifestation of the creed. But my informant was indignant that I should think there was little more to the matter than that.

Besides, he said, the phallic worship was purely allegorical. The marriage of young girls to older, or even old, men is a common feature of some Indian religions and enjoys the full approval of many educated and sincere people. Yet I often think such customs, sanctioned as they are by time and habit, are more the result of convenience and the power of human instincts and natural desires than of any true loyalty to a doctrine.

The Tantras worship God or *Brahma* the Creator of the Universe. Unlike the conventional Western churchgoer who finds it easier to visualize God as a person or a kind of elder statesman figure residing in heaven, than to experience Him as a creative and life-giving force, the Tantras avoid any attempt to personify God, or to give God a recognizable identity. They do not ascribe He, or She or It to Brahma because Brahma is the one generative and creating being that cannot be a human being or have human form.

On the other hand, all human attributes are attributes of God for everything is God. All experiences, the objects we see, the material things we make, the imaginary objects we invent are divine manifestations of God for God alone creates. Since God has no form, say the Tantras, we are free to label God in whatever way we wish and therefore to assign any sex to God. In fact they identify the Deity with *both* sexes

The nearest they come to personifying God is to see God as the Mother (*Shakti*) and Father (*Shiva*) of all creation. One God, but a dualistic God; not two interdependent and coexisting Gods but a combination of female and male forces. Among humans and the animal world alike Mother expresses love, kindliness, the gentle side of nature; Father expresses the energy or driving force.

Strangely, it is in this polarization detail that the Hindu and Buddhist Tantrics differ, for the poles are given the reverse characteristics in Hindu Tantra, the male being the passive partner and the female the active. Both traditions, however, see the *Shakti-Shiva* combination as the universal creating force which generates life and matter, and the Tantras liken the divine act of creation of the universe to sexual coition. It seems logical, since this is the only way we know of creating life.

Hence the phallic idols, the *linga* and the *yoni* which are, respectively, the representations of the male and female sex organs and which form the center of Tantric spiritual life. The idols are often realistic in detail, carved in wood or polished stone and can be life size or of giant proportions; sometimes they are ornately carved with patterns or scenes.

It is not uncommon for some Tantras, the Lingayat Hindus, to possess a personal linga made of metal or stone and carry it about on their person as a kind of talisman. In temples or village shrines the linga and yoni are normally depicted together to symbolize the union which is the creating force and therefore truly representative of God.

Certainly I felt the idea of a dualistic God showing the way to monism made some sense. Shiva and Shakti are inseparable in Tantric tradition as the two aspects of God as heat is inseparable from fire, light from illumination, mass from energy, matter from force, male from female. But my learned lama was at pains to emphasize it is not the carved phallus itself that is worshipped—this was merely a visual aid—but the dual Shiva and Shakti force represented by its union with the female counterpart.

Tantrism is one of the very ancient religions of India; its origin is far back in the past. Little has been written down and its teaching is invariably passed on by gurus who hold a special place in the life of the faith and play a key role in its perpetuation. An initiate cannot begin his indoctrination without the guidance of a guru and he certainly cannot find the ultimate reality of transcendence without one.

Nor must he look on his guru as a mere human teacher, a learned man who has the ability to impart his knowledge. The guru must be adored and waited on as the representative of the Deity, even as the Deity itself in human form. And the guru, of course, must be one who has already realized in himself the Truth. It is said that mere learning remains mental and ritual becomes mechanical unless energized by the personality of the guru.

This communication of impulsion from guru to disciple or initiate is done by means of a *mantra*, a mystic loaded word, a sound or syllable with which the mind can be occupied to the exclusion of all else and which is carefully chosen by the guru to match the initiate's individual personality, temperament, physical health and other personal factors. The mantra, repeated over and over again, becomes a sacred power to which is joined the power of the guru.

Worship itself is of two kinds, inner and outer, both with the object of identification with God. An initiate must believe the Deity can only be truly worshiped by his becoming the Deity. Inner worship is mental and mystic in character and exhibits no outward sign; it involves meditation and yoga to an extreme degree. Outer forms of worship include the physical factors with offerings, the burning of incense, singing. Inner worship awakens hidden faculties in man and in Tantric tradition can only be learned from a guru.

Much importance is attached in the ritual to chakras which are vital centers of consciousness sited at various points in the body, each responsible for an area of human significance. In meditation under the guru's influence these centers can be opened up and activated to lead the initiate to reach full knowledge and transcendence.

I could not discover the full extent to which eroticism was employed in Tantric rites, and much of what I did find out was not relevant to the purpose of my search, though it is clear that sexual union is of principal significance. In some mystic rituals in which the sexual act is used by the initiate—with or without a woman present, I gathered—the act is not carried through to its natural conclusion but is so controlled by power of will that no actual emission occurs. The male surge is contained so that the seed disperses within the body and rises to the top of the head where it dissolves to become an uncreated force which fills the initiate with bliss. I wondered what a doctor might have to say about practices of this sort.

The Tantras set great store by a variety of ritual forms of worship designed to strengthen devotional power and concentration. Self-restraint, will power, the force of intellect and singleness of mind in the face of severe temptations of the flesh are claimed to lead the follower to a spiritual plane in which his occult and yogic powers become highly developed. There is ample evidence that there is more than a grain of truth in the claims.

But without wishing to appear skeptical or to pass a lofty and ill-informed judgment on an ancient and little-understood religion, with which I acquainted myself only slightly in passing, I was inclined nevertheless to dismiss the Tantric cults as mere heathen survivals in a modern world. They are objects of curiosity, vastly interesting and, I believe, worth the attention I have given them but of little use in practice.

There is a good deal more to the subject than I have set down. I dare say there was more to it than I was told about during my on-the-spot brief investigation at Benares, but rightly or wrongly I felt that to dig deeper into this mysterious area of human experience would lead me precisely nowhere.

Peace should be a simple matter. If the Tantras found true enlightenment, surely they went about it in a very complicated way.

12

A Month in the Forest

WHAT I had seen and heard in the past few weeks had been what I would call "interesting documentary." The scenes were rich in color and excitement, the practices weird and eye-catching, the philosophies interesting, if sometimes a little bewildering. All in all they contributed a miscellany of fascinating data to my work file and I knew I would be able to look back on the events I had witnessed and places I had visited with the pleasure of a dedicated tourist.

The trouble was, I did not set out to be a tourist. My quest was to find the source of peace, the right circumstances for achieving a quiet mind. My job had taken me to many out-of-the-way corners of the globe and it was not for fresh scenery that I was searching.

If this verdict seems to disregard or reject too coldly any possible value in the forms of Buddhist and Hindu worship I had investigated perhaps I have stated the situation with more vigor than it deserves. But I was fairly well convinced that for my purposes the value of my travelogue journey to Northern India lay in the fact that it enabled me to eliminate much of what it had to offer. My inquiries would have been less than thorough if I had ignored the possible avenues which Benares, Sarnath and Kathmandu presented.

When I got back to Bangkok I decided to seek out the Venerable Buddhadasa Bhikkhu and lay my problem before him. I had heard a great deal about this remarkable man who was a leader of the Buddhism in Thailand. There seemed to be two sides to the expression of his vocation; not only was he Thailand's leading Buddhist monk and a highly respected member of the establishment and exponent of orthodox Buddhism, he was also a strenuous advocate of "pure

Buddhism" and was at pains to teach the original, unadulterated concepts of Buddhist thinking to those who came to him for personal guidance.

I am not in the least implying any criticism of Buddhadasa Bhikkhu for his "double-barreled" conduct of the religious life of his flock. The conventional sermons he delivered were based on the needs and the traditional beliefs of the population and anything else would have been unacceptable. Almost every religion in the world today suffers from the same inhibition—the public's need of a popularized version of their indigenous religion.

Although I had read published extracts of Buddhadasa Bhikkhu's lectures and sermons on the conventional Theravāda doctrine and found them to be fairly commonplace expositions, I knew there was more to Buddhism, and more to Buddhadasa Bhikkhu. It was with a good deal of optimism, therefore, that I fixed up to go and see him.

Buddhadasa Bhikkhu (Buddhadasa means the servant of Buddha and Bhikkhu literally means beggar but is the title of a monk), had established a monastery in the forest of Southern Thailand near the town of Chaiya in the district of Surat Thani, the area where Buddhism is reputed to have been introduced to Thailand.

I cleared my desk and set off with the intention of staying at Suan Mok until I had found out everything I could about the original raw, basic beliefs and teachings of Buddha, uncluttered, unmodernized, unpopularized.

I arrived at the temple grounds just as the monks were having their pre-noon meal, the last food of the day. A group of about twelve were sitting on the ground in a dilapidated old wooden shelter and among them I immediately recognized Buddhadasa from photographs I had seen of him.

He was a man in his sixties, plump, fairly tall for a Thai with alert, intelligent eyes behind small, round spectacles with narrow black rims. When the meal was over and Buddhadasa had finished talking to his attentive audience I approached him and introduced myself.

He greeted me warmly and listened to my reasons for visiting him and my interest in learning about his teachings. He invited me to stay with him in the temple grounds for as long as I wished and discuss with him any matters that interested me. It was to be one of the most useful episodes of my entire search.

"Come, I will show you your living quarters," he said. I followed him deep into the woods and eventually came upon a small cottage completely surrounded by dense forest. It had been built by a wealthy business man who had visited the monastery, he told me, and after using it for his stay had made a present of it for the use of other visitors. Buddhadasa then led the way down a narrow track and showed me a mountain stream which was to be my source of water for drinking and bathing.

"You will be able to relax here and your mind will become quiet," Buddhadasa said. "When you have settled down I will come and speak with you."

With these words the plump, yellow-robed figure of the Venerable Buddhadasa Bhikkhu scurried off into the undergrowth and returned to the temple, leaving me to my own devices in the heart of the unfamiliar forest, utterly alone. I looked about me and all I could see were trees and tangled vegetation; the only sounds were the buzz of insects and the shouting of the forest birds.

The sun was still high and the air was warm. This was surely living close to nature; I looked forward to the prospect of spending a leisurely few weeks in the quiet, peaceful atmosphere of Suan Mok. The situation suited me very well.

Suddenly I had an uneasy feeling that I was not alone, that I was being watched. I looked up. In the trees above my head a family of monkeys were staring at me with large suspicious eyes, they evidently regarded my intrusion on their territory as a matter worthy of investigation but in the days that followed we became quite accustomed to each other's company.

Inside the cottage there were a few simple items of furniture but little else. I placed my belongings on the table and set off to reconnoiter the countryside. My time was my own. There was nothing to hurry for. The grounds of Suan Mok were beautiful and from time to time I stopped to breathe in the atmosphere and just gaze at the scene. On one such occasion I became aware of an acute stinging sensation in my big toe. I looked down to find a colony of huge ants scrambling over my sandaled foot and making a meal of my toe on the way.

At Suan Mok there were, I suppose, about twenty-five resident monks as well as a handful of lay visitors like myself. I spoke to one or two of the monks but the main delight of the place was its solitude and I don't suppose they were any more anxious to engage in conversation than I was. It was wholly conducive to contemplation and meditation.

One of the interesting people I met during those first few days was a former engineer who, like me, had come for a short visit and then decided to remain at Suan Mok away from the hectic life of the city. He occupied himself with various building jobs in the retreat including the setting up of a gravity-fed water pumping system. He had installed electrical facilities and often spent his spare time carrying out repairs to motor vehicles, all the while immersing himself as much as he could in Buddhadasa's teaching.

I came across a museum that was being constructed to display early scenes of Buddha's activities. In one section of it a group of monks were busy making cement reliefs depicting Buddhist scenes. They were working from photographs Buddhadasa had acquired in India. He believed that much of the Thai Buddhist art was of relatively recent origin in comparison with Indian and was therefore not as accurate in its representation of the activities of Buddha as they actually occurred. And he was a stickler for accuracy. The point about the museum, I was told, was that it would present symbolically but as accurately as possible scenes from the life of the Buddha. Also in progress was the construction of a number of small huts and facilities for visiting pilgrims to stay in while making a refuge in the area.

There was a story that Buddhadasa's passion for no-nonsense Buddhism had led him into a slight brush with the law when he called for an end to the use of "spirit houses." These are a traditional feature of Thai life and are supposed to provide protection from the spirits of the dead. Like a small house very ornate, exquisitely carved and painted in bright orange, gold and white and mounted on a concrete pedestal outside one's front door they offer shelter for any wayward spirit that might otherwise enter the house.

Buddhadasa's view that such superstitious rubbish had no place in authentic Buddhist lore affronted many people and an attempt was made to arrest the learned monk on the grounds that such an attack on traditional beliefs encouraged Communism. The matter was eventually allowed to drop.

Scattered throughout the temple grounds were huts in which the monks, who had built them with their own hands, lived and meditated alone amid the serenity of nature. The whole setting was perfect for the purpose. My walks through the forest, watching monkeys and gibbons jumping about the treetops, beautiful multicolored birds in flight, snakes sliding gracefully through the leaves (which meant you had to carry a stick with you at all times), and the armies of ants chasing back and forth between sources of food and their underground homes, all had the therapeutic effect of tranquilizing my active mind.

I found the temple grounds of Suan Mok and the whole environment utterly different from the atmosphere of fanaticism and ritual in Nepal. But I saw nothing of Buddhadasa Bhikkhu himself and I formed the impression that he must be avoiding me and purposely making himself scarce. He knew I had come to his retreat with a large number of questions on my mind. I came to the conclusion he wanted me to relax my mental faculties and quieten down before engaging in any conversation. He believed that in solitude silence comes and fills your being.

I had been there more than a week before I saw him again after our first encounter. I was sitting at the porch of my cottage when I heard the rustle of approaching footsteps. He emerged from the forest wearing a wide smile and carrying an armful of books. But he didn't stop to talk. He stayed just long enough to suggest I might like to do some reading and departed as quickly as he had arrived.

Once again I was on my own, with the difference that now I had at least a small library of literature as a companion as well as the monkeys. Presumably the teacher had decided that I was by this time in the right state of mind to begin studying. I examined the titles and found the books were all concerned with Zen Buddhism. I had heard Zen referred to by some of the monks as a subject frequently used by Buddhadasa in instructing his disciples. I felt I could now make some progress.

Several days passed and the quiet life continued as before except that I was now applying myself to my subject. Life was very good. My food was brought to me by Buddhadasa's young nephew, fresh fruit, various curries, chopped meat, fish and vegetables—there was no strictly vegetarian diet here—all of it provided by the local villagers or cooked by the temple's two women cooks when free offerings ran short.

I ate breakfast and lunch but after that nothing more, with the possible exception of drinks, until breakfast the following day. I made a friend, a young man from Thailand's Government Rice Department who was spending three months at Suan Mok prior to getting married and whom, because he had shaved his head, I nicknamed Curly much to everyone's amusement.

Then, quite suddenly, I began to see more of Buddhadasa Bhikkhu. He invited me to his quarters for discussions which lasted from thirty minutes to an hour in the evenings. I found his philosophy very much in tune with my own thinking. His message was clear. Like that of the great Krishnamurti it was a plea that we should experience life directly instead of blindly following teachings based on the secondhand experiences of others.

"We humans are like fish who do not see the water surrounding them," said Buddhadasa. "We usually do not notice life going on around us because we have become so accustomed to it. It is obvious, self-evident and perpetual and we therefore never really spend any time on becoming truly aware of its nature as a continuing process."

Buddhadasa explained his approach to awareness by stating that a constant state of meditation should be integrated with all the day's activities…"eating, drinking, working, sleeping, walking through the forest, watching the monkeys, bathing, listening to the stream, watching the clouds drift across the sky." The meaning of life was to be found in experience rather than in generalizations…"understanding seeps through during the common activities of daily life."

A basic tenet of his doctrine was his strong objection to the conventional dualistic approach to the manifestations of life: the rightness of one thing and the wrongness of another. He had symbolized this prominently in the Center of the temple area by means of a huge construction of the *Yin* and *Yang* symbols denoting the opposites good and evil, black and white. The monks had arranged black and white stones in the form of a great circle with an S-shaped division across the center, black stones occupying one side and white the other. In Zen symbolism when the circle is set in motion, as all facets of life are in motion, the black and white merge into grey "thereby freeing us from the preposterous blindness of duality which had held

Western man in its grip since Plato."

Zen looks upon the dualistic distinctions as useless human inventions. Good and evil, flesh and spirit, truth and falsehood, finite and infinite, material and spiritual, eternal and temporal, subject and object, are all illusory distinctions.

During my month-long stay at Suan Mok I had many conversations with Buddhadasa Bhikkhu and it was a refreshing experience. I could clearly see why the man, although highly revered by his Thai Buddhist followers, was regarded as very much a rebel because of his condemnation of so many of the present-day Buddhist practices which man has evolved down the centuries to satisfy his ignorance.

He offered no formal program of training yet his message was clear and at the and of my stay I felt my pursuit of the quiet mind was now bringing definite results. My series of brief but valuable meetings with Buddhadasa certainly conditioned me for experiences which were to follow.

13

With Suzuki in Japan

MY first glimpse of Zen was a tantalizing one. Did it hold the secret of clear understanding of life and so of the path to a quiet mind? The man who had brought me that first encounter with a faith about which I had read much and seen little was one who seemed to have at his fingertips the solution to many of the problems of the spirit; if Buddhadasa Bhikkhu himself was an example of its benefits then Zen was demonstrably a philosophy which demanded further inquiry. I determined to investigate the field more thoroughly at the first opportunity.

A few months later I had a job to do in Japan and when I arrived in Tokyo I telephoned Dr. Suzuki, the world's foremost authority on Zen. He had written more than a dozen books on the subject in English. He was fluent in German, French and English in addition to his native Japanese and one section of his house was filled to the brim with books in these languages on a wide variety of subjects.

I was able to fix an appointment and caught a train to Kita Kamakura, just south of Tokyo, where Suzuki lived in a typical Japanese-style house perched on the side of the hill overlooking the town.

I was met by his secretary, an attractive Japanese American girl, who led me to his study. Without her I doubt if we should have made any headway in the conversation that followed, or even whether Dr. Suzuki and I would have made any contact at all, for the sage was over ninety at the time and so hard of hearing that I had to yell at the top of my voice in order to communicate with him.

Each word I uttered was repeated by the girl in English for it seemed Dr. Suzuki could understand her voice frequencies and not mine. I had spent some time in Japan after the war doing photography and recording work at the International War Trials and was able to speak a little Japanese: I tried it out on Dr. Suzuki but in the end we reverted to English as spoken by me and reiterated by his secretary. It worked much better.

For all his years Dr. Suzuki had a boyish charm and an extremely quick mind and I had to summon every ounce of concentration to keep up with him. This interesting little man with large bushy eyebrows and a brain sharp as steel had a peculiar way of answering questions: he threw the question back in such a way that the questioner got a glimpse of himself and that way discovered the fundamental directness of life.

The few hours spent with Dr. Suzuki over several pots of green tea gave me more insight to Zen than all the numerous books I had read on the subject in my Suan Mok hideaway.

"What are the basic essentials of Zen?" I asked.

"The essentials of Zen doctrine can never be accurately and fully described because they are an experience and not a set of ideas," he replied.

Western tradition had two major influences: the Hebraic and the Greek based on the philosophies of Plato and Socrates. Both were basically dualistic. The limits of human reason needed to recognize the essential paradox of reason. Zen had nothing to do with complex abstractions of the intellect. There is a need to accept what is—as a matter of fact. Accept or not, it still is.

"In Zen it is the living fact—not the abstract or intellectual truth but the lived truth—that counts," he said. "To know Zen, even to begin to understand it, it is necessary to practise it. Facts must be faced without thinking about them, they must be directly experienced."

Dr. Suzuki explained that the aim of Zen was enlightenment or *satori*, an immediate, unreflected insight into reality without rationalization or intellectualization, the relation of oneself to the Universe.

"This new experience is the innocent pre-intellectual, immediate grasp of a child but on a different level," he said. "The level of the full development of man's reason, individuality and objectivity.

While the child's experience of oneness comes before the experience of duality, in enlightenment it lies after it."

This aim, he said, implies the elimination of greed in all forms, whether for fame, possessions or affection. One needs to be an authority to oneself and not submit to or seek understanding from others. Deliverance must be right where you are.

"A business man lives his life in awakened awareness. If he fails to do so he will not be a successful business man. Our true natures are always working, but because of our preoccupation with success, wealth, prestige, intellectual superiority, we never see it. We must empty our minds to free them from false values and directly experience our real selves."

Dr. Suzuki pointed out that while the aim of psychoanalysis was to make the unconscious conscious or to replace the id by the ego what distinguishes Zen from the other religions and systems is the quality of being attached and not attached, the state of attachment yet without attachment. "Finite is infinite, infinite is finite. When you understand this you understand Zen."

Dr. Suzuki emphasized that rational knowledge plays an important role in life and science has contributed greatly to man's benefit however it has dulled his access to intuitive wealth.

"Man does not become free from the intricacies of life by withdrawing into the seclusion of a temple or 'dropping out'. He must be both spectator and participant. A scientist possesses much background knowledge gained from assiduous application to his subject but this knowledge blooms into creativity during moments of silence."

He made the point that lying dormant in all of us are latent creative and benevolent powers. Because of ignorance we are generally unaware of these powers. Zen could dispel this ignorance and open doors to an infinitely blessed life.

Suzuki went on to spell out for me the basic differences in Eastern and Western mentality and why Zen, itself so simple, was a difficult philosophy for the Western mind to grasp. In the East, he said, before an artist paints a tree he "becomes" that tree. A poet will identify himself with what he is describing. To illustrate the point he drew a comparison between the great seventeenth century Japanese poet Basho and Tennyson.

A poem by Basho went:

> When I look carefully
> I see the *mazuna* blooming
> by the hedge!

Taking a book from one of the shelves which lined the room, he opened it at a marked page and recited these lines of Tennyson:

> Flower in the crannied wall
> I pluck you out of the crannies;
> Hold you here, root and all, in my hand,
> Little flower—but if I could understand
> What you are, root and all, and all in all,
> I should know—what God and man is.

Basho loved nature and was probably walking along a road when he noticed the insignificant wild *mazuna* in the hedgerow and immediately felt one with it. Most Westerners separate themselves from nature, and while valuing it for its usefulness in providing food for themselves and their farm animals, and no doubt admiring it for its beauty, nevertheless feel themselves to be on a totally different and superior plane and in no sense to be equated with it.

To the Easterner nature is much more. It is within him, as much a part of him as his friends, his neighbors, the birds, the animals. And it was this fellow-feeling for nature which so excited Basho's poetic instincts when he noticed the inconspicuous weed, innocent and unpretentious, not expecting or desiring to be noticed. He saw it in its full heavenly glory and its very humbleness evoked his admiration. Basho, too, was filled with a divine love which transcended human feeling and detected greatness in the smallest thing.

Tennyson, typical Westerner that he is, plucks his flower out by the roots and stares at it with an almost botanical intensity. He must have felt emotions like Basho's for his gaze inspired the poetic muse in him also, but his analytical brain is stirred into action first. He must dissect the plant and find out all about it. Basho does not pick the flower and kill it; he just looks, absorbed in his thoughts which he does not bother to express. While he regards the weed in silence, Tennyson is philosophizing: "If I could understand you I would know what God is."

Basho holds no such inquisition; he feels within himself all the mysteries of the mazuna plant and has no desire to turn the experience into an intellectual exercise. He lets an exclamation mark speak for him.

In his poem, said Suzuki, Tennyson does not identify himself with either God or nature. With a typical Western approach he separates himself from both and regards the flower with scientific objectivity. Basho is absolutely subjective. He sees the flower and for all he knows the flower sees him, it is part of life, part of him.

And it is the to us very unintelligibility of this statement and this kind of experience which points up the difference between Eastern and Western minds. The East is silent and introspective and meditative. The West is intellectual and analytical. And far from displaying stupidity or dullness of mind the silence of the East can be extremely eloquent, said Suzuki.

To Westerners the ways of the East often appear stupid or at best inscrutable. The typical Easterner is not so demonstrative, he does not always show obvious evidence of intelligence, he appears unmoved, unenthusiastic, indifferent. Easterners realize, however, that without this indifference their native intelligence would not permit them to live together harmoniously. In the East there is never a rigid demarcation line between what is white and what is black.

Mulling over the famous philosopher's words later I tried to apply what he had told me to a factor in the world scene which has most of us worried now—including the Russians—namely the inscrutable behavior of the Chinese, whose numbers total a quarter of the earth's population. Their expanding power constitutes the greatest threat to peace the world has ever known. What goes on in *their* minds? And would a comparative examination of Eastern and Western mentalities help us to reconcile their extreme and apparently irrational conduct today with what was once a noble and proud cultural and religious heritage?

Do the Chinese, chanting the thoughts of Chairman Mao, have quiet minds? And if they haven't, with their background and the kind of Eastern mind which Dr. Suzuki had so eloquently explained, why haven't they? My guess is they have.

Very little now leaks out to the rest of the world about the activities of this vast nation of seven hundred million souls, and what does reach our ears we don't like; the cruel pranks of the so-called Red Guard of unscrupulous youth of both sexes, the heartless incarceration of innocent Westerners, the stories of schoolchildren taught to hate by their Communist teachers under a regime which seems to have world domination as its destiny.

In one aspect the Chinese are already one jump ahead of the rest: they have us puzzled. But this surely is only an example of the way in which they are turning what is part of the Oriental character to their own advantage. From the time of Marco Polo the Chinese people have been an enigma. Now, under the poet-dictator Mao with his inexplicable motives and his sinister-seeming influence over the entire race, they have formed themselves into a veritable flood of malevolent and dedicated nonthinking people anti-everything and anti-everyone. Their mood, the purpose of which is so far undefined with any precision but nonetheless alarming, defies comprehension by the Westerner with his analytical mind and his predilection for rationality and logic.

The Chinese personality is made up of part Confucianism and part Taoism but both the Confucian and the Taoist philosophies were heavily influenced by Buddhism and thus the Chinese are something of an amalgam of all three. The Taoist side of their character abhors violence and leads them to follow a motto of courtesy first, hostility second.

In war as in personal relationships they will avoid pushing an opponent to the wall for they realize a trapped animal fights. Tai Chi, the forerunner of judo, was used by Taoists for it enabled the Taoist to turn his opponent's strength to his own advantage. The virtuous Confucian ethics seem to have gone by the board under the Mao regime but the Communist Chinese have retained the tactics of Taoism and employed them with success in foreign relations.

Since Communism put down roots in China there has been a constant struggle between the Taoists and Confucian elements. Years ago it would have seemed impossible that such codes could exist alongside Communism but the situation is all too plain for everyone to see. And I put this down to the influence of another ancient Chinese character trait: that to them the shortest distance between two points is not a straight line but the route of least resistance. It is this, and the struggle between opposing philosophies which have molded the Chinese character over a period of centuries, that has brought about the tremendous upheaval of the past few years.

It is quite understandable that the Chinese methods of achieving world domination, if that is their aim, should differ from those of Moscow. The Russians positively enjoy a show of force when they consider it necessary to make their point. The callous invasion of Czechoslovakia and suppression of free thought there was a good example. Even at a time when the Russians were doing all in their power to build up commerce with Western countries, and when their relations abroad were buoyant, they did not shrink from the use of a few battalions of heavy artillery to crush a satellite which was wandering off course.

The Chinese, with their long civilization and its emphasis on the humanities, would do better than that. They are past masters in practical psychology and depend far more than the Russians upon persuasion.

Chairman Mao himself put it in a nutshell when describing tactics for guerrilla warfare. "Enemy advances, we retreat. Enemy retreats, we pursue. Enemy encamps, we disturb. Enemy tires out, we attack." War is a kind of chess game they like to win, but not by head-on assault. Victory is to be accomplished, but through the use of brain, not brawn.

Another ancient stunt is *li chien*, which means sowing discord. It has proved a powerful weapon in the hands of the Chinese Communists, who used it to exploit the contradictions among their opponents, winning over the neutrals and crushing their enemies, with the unwitting help of the neutrals. The neutrals, of course, become the enemies of tomorrow, to be dealt with later!

In fact, the more one probes the Chinese mental processes the more disturbing the prospects become. If we in the West are worried because of a Chinese puzzle we cannot unravel, how much more worried or alarmed would we be if we could read all the signs fluently? Meanwhile the people of China are waiting, and we must be on our guard.

Dr. Suzuki's illuminating description of the basic differences between the mentalities of West and East reminded me of the time when I first arrived in Thailand. I found the people strange and illogical and thought I would never be able to understand their behavior, which frequently defied what I considered to be common sense. It was only after I had studied their religion for a time that I began to understand their mentality, which is steeped in thousands of years of religious influence.

They have an expression, *mai pen rai*, which means something like "never mind." It was so commonly used whenever things didn't go as planned that we Westerners used to refer to Thailand as *mai pen rai* land.

The Thais would tackle a job with enthusiasm and with all the effort they could muster. If all did not go well they would not think in terms of failure and get upset. They would say "Mai pen rai"—and get on with the next job.

At first I thought it must show the Thais were indolent or just plain irresponsible. I thought mai pen rai must be their equivalent of the Mexicans' mañana. But later I saw the innate intelligence associated with mai pen rai and developed a deep respect for both the expression and the Thai people who were able to use it so freely.

My brief visit with Dr. Suzuki not only provided me with the opportunity to meet a remarkable and extraordinary man but also left me with a clear appreciation of Zen Buddhist principles which fitted in quite closely with what I had already learned to date of Buddhism, the original, clear teaching of Buddha. Suzuki himself, lucid, sharp witted, perhaps one of the last of the old medieval-type "wise men" and wholly at one with the world, had been frank and as helpful as he was able to be.

I cherish the memory of our interview all the more since it must have been one of the last he gave. A short time afterwards I read newspaper reports that he was dead.

There is a story of Dr. Suzuki attending a conference on Zen and psychoanalysis. As a guest of honour he sat at the front table. He was then eighty-six and during one particularly long session he was thought to be asleep.

He sat immobile, eyes closed, unperturbed by events going on in the room, but when a breeze scattered some papers down the table it was Suzuki's hand that flashed out and secured them after they had swept past the others sitting with him. Suzuki had been in meditation, delicately balanced between relaxed detachment and instant alertness.

The anecdote reminds me of the time when I was serving as a recruit in the United States Army. One young chap, much to the aggravation of the instructors, always fell asleep during lectures and demonstrations. He was constantly being punished for his lack of interest in his studies, yet at examination time he consistently achieved high scores. It wasn't long before the instructors came to accept the man's annoying idiosyncrasies in exchange for the satisfaction of having a student with perfect papers.

D.T. Suzuki 1870-1966

When Suzuki spoke of higher stages of consciousness he spoke as a man who dwelt therein and the impression he made on those he met was that they too, of their own volition, must enter the fringes of this state instead of seeking for the intellectual symbols to describe a state of awareness which lies indeed beyond the intellect.

I asked Dr. Suzuki if there were any living persons in the Western world who were in contact with reality. He mentioned Krishnamurti who, although Indian, spent most of his time in the West. He also mentioned Thomas Merton the Trappist monk and author of many books including the famous *No Man Is An Island.*

123

Before I left Suzuki he gave me the names of several Zen masters in Tokyo who spoke English and advised me to meet them. He also recommended a visit to the Shokoku Temple in Northern Kyoto if time allowed. My visit to Japan was cut short, however, and I was unable to do as he suggested. But in the back of my mind I decided that Shokoku was the next place to pursue my search, and on a subsequent visit to Japan I made a point of realizing this intention.

14

The Secrets of Zen

KYOTO is one of the more beautiful cities of Japan and was for centuries the country's capital. It contains many interesting buildings including San-ju-san-gen-du, the temple of 33,333 images of Kwannon, the goddess of mercy. I was sorely tempted to explore the town for I knew there was much to see, but I was in a hurry to pursue my inquiries and excited at the prospect of exploring the mysteries of Zen at the famous temple of Shokoku which Dr. Suzuki had told me about.

I had flown from Bangkok to Tokyo and covered the 330 miles to Kyoto by train. I booked in at a hotel and had a good night's rest in preparation for my visit to the temple the following day. After breakfast I hired a cab and told the driver where I wanted to go.

The temple lay on a stretch of flat ground in the north of the city. The taxi driver dropped me off at the heavy wooden gates and I went in with the intention of browsing round the temple area, and if possible finding someone who could tell me the sort of things that went on there.

Inside the gates I found myself in a large compound surrounded by dried mud walks. There were extensive gardens and bamboo groves and a number of temples each with its own gate and walls. In the center of the compound was what appeared to be a lecture hall of impressive dimensions. I went in.

The first sight that met my eyes was a huge ferocious-looking dragon painted in red and gold on the ceiling. I learned later the story of this dragon. The artist who was commissioned to paint it told the temple authorities he didn't know what a dragon looked like. He was advised to meditate "on becoming a dragon." After three months of persistent meditation he was able to paint the ceiling.

The room was in silence. At the far end, raised on a high platform, sat a large gold Buddha image. As I stood there gazing at the spectacle and soaking up the atmosphere I heard a slight movement and turned to see a figure approaching me from a corner of the room.

I imagine the inhabitants of the temple must be fairly used to sightseers for the monk, as the man turned out to be, greeted me with a smile and immediately volunteered the information that the hall we were standing in was used only for an occasional ritual. I found he spoke a little English so I explained why I was there. He seemed very interested and at once put himself in charge of my further education.

"Over here beyond the bell tower," he said, "is the gate which leads to the training school for Zen monks."

I asked him if it was permitted for visitors to enter the gate and see the monks at their training. He said he would take me through and explain anything I wished to know; what I did not see for myself he would tell me about. I said I was considering taking a course in Zen myself so that I could penetrate its mysteries and try to understand its teaching at first hand.

"The courses last for a year or more," he replied. I was completely taken aback at this and he laughed, though not unkindly, at my expression of surprise.

"Where do the students go when they have been through the course?" I asked.

"Most of them, when they have completed their studies, will become monks at other Shokoku temples scattered throughout Japan," he said. "Others, after years of meditation and *koan* study and study of philosophy will become Zen masters."

The life of a student of Zen at the Shokoku temple was monastic and austere but I formed the impression that it was not too arduous or demanding except insofar as the requirements of self-discipline and periods of meditation were concerned. In these matters the instructors were strict. Laymen who agree to observe the rules of the monastery life are allowed to participate, particularly at the evening meditation sessions, but I was disappointed that I was not going to be able to delve as deeply into the subject as I would have liked.

"Tell me more about the life of the temple," I asked my guide. "The daily routine and program of study. What are the objectives?"

"The object of Zen is to reach satori or enlightenment," he said. "And this is done principally through the koan exercise and *zazen*. The koan is used instrumentally for opening the mind to its own secrets. The koan is neither a riddle nor a witty remark, but it sounds nonsensical upon hearing or reading. It has as its objective to arouse doubt and pushes the mind to its farthest limit.

"It is a puzzle which cannot be solved by logical thinking; one must go beyond thinking into intuition. The more you think the more puzzled the mind becomes. Then the mind discovers its inadequacy in its attempt to solve an insoluble problem; the futility of effort is realized and the mind becomes quiet."

So the object of Zen was my object: a quiet mind.

"I will give you a simple example of koan," the monk went on, "so that you will be able to follow my meaning more clearly. A student asks "What is Buddha?" "The cat is climbing the post," answers the instructor. "But I do not understand." "Ask the post," is the reply.

"The Zen student is warned not to try to gain the meaning of the koan from the wording, or to permit his imagination to seek the answer or to try to find a solution through logical analysis. He is rather expected to use the koan as an instrument. Zen meditation is no meditation. If other thoughts interfere they are not to be struggled with; one simply returns to the koan. The aim is to keep the koan before the mind regardless of what one is doing. When other matters intrude on the mind come back to the koan. When all appears hopeless and a period of supreme frustration is experienced one may be approaching the moment of realization. Only when reason ceases does sudden intuitive enlightenment occur."

This made sense to me. I could see how such methods, involving the imposition upon the intellect of an apparently irrational or nonsensical set of thoughts, would force the mind into a quiet state. If one was lucky (or perhaps well tuned by much experience and practice of koan exercises), such a dialogue would bring about satori and instantaneous recognition, beyond words, of new depth and meaning.

"And you just mentioned zazen. What is meant by zazen?" I asked.

"Zazen means sitting cross-legged in deep, quiet meditation and serves to help in the solving of the koan. The practice of zazen is secondary to the solution of the koan," he said.

My informant went on to describe the life of the temple. A few weeks are set aside each year for the more mundane chores of monastic life such as tending the gardens of the temple area, doing carpentry jobs and so on. During the first week of May the spring concentration sessions start. The two main buildings in which the lessons are given are the central hall, the first building I had entered when I arrived at the Shokoku temple, and the *zendo* or meditation hall.

They are connected by a covered pathway of stone about fifty yards long.

The Shokoku meditation hall is reputed to be one of the largest and finest in Japan. It is built on a raised stone terrace with a stone walk around the perimeter; the building is of unpainted wood with a long overhanging roof and the interior is always dark, cool and quiet.

Inside, a raised wood platform skirts the base of the walls and on it are placed straw mats for the students to sit on. Hanging from the ceiling is a life-size statue of Kaspaya, a disciple of Buddha. In a room at the rear is a statue of the founder of Shokoku.

The course begins in the evening. The students enter the central hall and sit on the floor sipping green tea and during this informal period the instructor comes into the hall unobtrusively. When he has the students' attention he reads the rules of the temple establishment and reminds everyone of the hard work which lies ahead. The group then moves off to the meditation hall for a short period of meditation before turning in for the night on their mats on the meditation platform.

At 3 a.m. a bell is rung and the lights of the meditation hall are switched on. In silence the would-be monks roll up their blankets and fold them away out of sight, then proceed to a bathroom where they wash their faces in cold water. They return to the mats on which they spent the night and sit upright in the cross-legged zazen attitude. The teacher arrives and sits in his place. He lights a piece of incense and starts the day's activities by ringing a small hand bell and whacking together two hardwood blocks with a loud clap.

Several minutes of silence follow after which the group walks in procession to the central hall for an hour-long session of chanting. The prayers and incantations over, they return to the meditation hall for an hour of meditation. Breakfast is served: it consists of salty radish pickles and rice with cups of green tea. In the cold light of dawn the students eat their austere meal, then clean up the kitchen, the halls, the instructors' rooms and the garden.

By 7 a.m. most of the routine work is completed and the teacher invites those students cleaning the meditation hall to his private quarters for an informal chat, some more tea and a smoke. No one works very hard and time is found to bask in the morning sun and smoke a cigarette or two. At ten-thirty work stops and the students go to the kitchen for lunch, which is the main meal for the day.

The students then return to the meditation hall where they sit about informally, generally not talking though talking is not forbidden. At three o'clock the bell rings out again and this is the signal for the students to proceed to the central hall for the chanting of the afternoon sutras. They then go back once more to the meditation hall for further meditation before the evening meal. Everyone then washes out and dries his own eating bowl. And so the day draws on, always following the same pattern.

At dusk the students move silently into the meditation hall where lights are now burning dimly, and seat themselves cross-legged on cushions at their allocated positions on the raised platform round the edge of the room. At seven-thirty a monk sounds the big bell in the bell tower by ramming a hefty wooden beam at it with great force. As he does so he sings out a sutra which can be heard throughout the neighborhood. Now the main meditation sessions begin.

All is complete silence in the meditation hall. The teacher sits at the head of the room and the students meditate. There is no movement and the only sound is the gentle whisper of breathing. Suddenly, after about half an hour, there is a loud crash as the teacher whacks together the wood blocks. The students stand up and begin to circle the room in a walking meditation. They move slowly, like sleep walkers, round and round the room, until the teacher once again shatters the stillness with his pieces of wood and yells "Get out!"

The cry indicates a twenty minute rest interval but this is by no means the end of meditation for the day. Again the students return to their places and sit cross-legged on their mats for a further period of an hour during which no one must move a muscle. No doubt there are many sore joints while this test of will lasts but no one is allowed to move.

During this period the instructor walks round the room carrying a stick. If anyone shows signs of falling asleep through lack of physical activity he receives a light tap on the shoulder, then to be certain he is wide awake he gets four sharp blows on each side of his back. The slight pain inflicted is much less than the sound of impact would suggest, I was told.

The bell rings again and the walking meditation is resumed, but this time discipline is evidently less rigorous for several of the students are able to slip away and return with bowls of noodles which they consume rapidly before returning to their perambulations.

At ten-thirty the students are ready for another brief rest. They relax and have a cigarette. At eleven the bell rings again: it is time for the final sutras to be chanted. The lights of the hall are turned off and the students go into further meditation for an hour or two before turning in for the night. The next day's activities begin at 3 a.m. with the clanging of the bell.

So the days pass in the course of study for students of Zen Buddhism at the Shokoku Temple at Kyoto. The timetable, with its heavy emphasis on meditation, is rigid and visiting only to include the occasional lecture delivered by a visiting lecturer. For the most part instruction in the teachings of Zen is carried out in informal talks between the novitiates and their instructors.

Discipline within the temple confines is strict and I was uncomfortably aware during my brief stay of the fear, amounting almost to terror, in which the student population regard those in authority over them. And well they might, for I learned the severity of their treatment could sometimes reach fierce extremes.

It is not unusual for an erring student to be dragged bodily across the floor and thrashed with sticks to show him the error of his ways. An offender guilty of some relatively insignificant misdemeanor might find his brothers ganging up on him, and depending on the gravity of the crime, he might suffer a severe beating-up to bring him to his senses.

But despite the strictness I formed the impression that, provided the students conformed to what was expected of them and took their devotions seriously, the life was not unduly harsh. They performed all the menial tasks around the place, cleaning up, scrubbing floors, but the work was not hard labour and the even tenor of their routine was ideally suited to the purpose of their being there.

As for the merits of Zen philosophy itself, I was unable to probe deeply enough or gain by personal experience a proper spiritual insight into their intricacies. My time was limited for I was in Japan primarily on business. But I did find in conversations with my friendly guide and other monks at the temple—who fortunately included one of the English-speaking Zen masters about whom Dr. Suzuki had spoken—that the Buddhism followed was as authentic as any I had yet encountered.

The shock treatment approach was novel and I could appreciate that the koan system of jolting the mind into a state of quiet could be effective. But I'm sure it must take the ordinary lay follower of Zen a long time to grasp.

Whether it would have suited my personality or not I could not stay to find out, much to my regret. Nevertheless the practices and the serious, devout mood of Shokoku were impressive as was, by their very absence, the lack of theatrical ritual and demonstrative worshipping I had witnessed among the Buddhists in other areas in the East

It was about this time that I met and married my English wife. The trip we made to Europe soon after turned out to be well-timed, for there were interesting events brewing in the West, and particularly in Britain, which I wanted to investigate.

15

Transcendental Meditation versus "Pot"

IN the summer of 1967 a curious phenomenon was taking place: a tumultuous wave of enthusiasm for Transcendental Meditation was sweeping across the civilized Western world, and I was watching it with growing fascination and incredulity.

At the center of the fuss—it amounted almost to mass hysteria—was its most recent prophet on the scene, His Holiness the Maharishi Mahesh Yogi. The Maharishi was jetting between the European capitals and the United States drawing huge crowds of young people to his lectures. Wherever he went the newspapermen went too. He was photographed boarding and leaving planes; he was pictured surrounded by hippies and groups of flower people; he was interviewed at airports coming and going.

With his straggly flowing hair and beard, his beads, his simple white gown and sandals, his deerskin prayer mat and his infectious and disarming giggle, the Maharishi captured almost overnight the imagination of a whole generation as the latest embodiment of "love" and "peace." And at the same time he sparked off the scorn and the admiration, in about equal parts, of the parental generation and the clergy at the centers he visited.

Among his followers were the Beatles, still at the height of their fame as a pop group. It was a coup which brought him instant notoriety: what the Beatles did was news and the Maharishi Mahesh Yogi's name, as soon as people could pronounce it, became very big news. His progress through the lecture halls of Europe and the United States was attended by a wealth of coverage in the Press, some of it sceptical and cynical but all of it excellent publicity for the cult of meditation.

The Maharishi made his biggest incursion to date into the newspaper headlines when he addressed a conference in North Wales. Among his listeners were the Beatles, and, of course, hundreds of their fans. Said Paul McCartney: "We just came for a quiet weekend and look what happened."

Rolling Stone Mick Jagger was there with Marianne Faithfull. He gave as his reason for taking up meditation: "To be more at peace with myself and more at peace with the universe."

Beatle Paul said: "It's too good to be true, that's what it is. It's something for nothing." Another Beatle, John Lennon, fairly effervesced with enthusiasm. "The more people meditate the better. Maybe one day someone who meditates will become Prime Minister. If there's any possibility of getting this across it's worth it. At least it can't do any harm."

"Very right, very right," said the Maharishi with a giggle when he heard Lennon say this.

The seal of respectability was placed on the Maharishi's mission by no less a figure than the Archbishop of Canterbury, Dr. Michael Ramsey. Speaking at Bede Theological College in the North of England he declared there was a genuine analogy between the Christian forms of prayer and the Oriental meditations "recently adopted by the Beatles."

He did not believe contemplating as the last thing to concern ordinary men. Older generations were trained to think that plain Christian devotion is the thing that everyone should grasp but that mysticism is something very queer and abnormal and which is better left to a few experts and the last thing to talk about and practise.

"I think that is radically untrue and if anything the opposite of the truth," he said.

The Daily Sketch joined the ranks of the supporters. "Whatever he is Maharishi is a delightful personality. He has a sharp brain, argues brilliantly, sometimes with simple, direct stories, sometimes with far-out concepts. He bubbles over into laughter frequently. He tells the Beatles that the rich man is there to relieve the burdens of society. It is only difficult for a rich man to enter the kingdom of heaven if he just sits there and contemplates his wealth. 'Christ said the kingdom of heaven is within you and that is all I am saying'."

What was the message brought by the Maharishi which so captivated people? He said he had rediscovered the truth about life that had somehow been lost throughout the centuries.

"Happiness is what meditation offers here, now. It is so simple it would make you laugh. My message is about happiness and the search for happiness."

He explained the effect of meditation in these words: "If you dip a piece of cloth in yellow dye and put it out into the sun it dries a very faint yellow. When you dip the cloth again in the dye it dries a little stronger yellow. If you do it again and again, the dye will eventually dry fast, clear and strong until it is perfect. Your mind is like this piece of cloth, it reaches the ultimate of everything, cosmic consciousness."

Maharishi caused a stir wherever he went. He was interviewed by David Frost on television's Frost Report and on the BBC's Home Service he had a thirty minute conversation with Malcolm Muggeridge, who described his meditation philosophy as a pill "—a sort of spiritual capsule: take three drops and you'll be in tune with the infinite."

The Maharishi agreed. "Perhaps it takes only half a minute to take it, but the effect lasts many hours," he said.

"Presumably this must work for your followers," countered Muggeridge, "but what sort of people are they?"

"All kinds," said the Maharishi. "They include really responsible men in society and those who want to progress in the world."

The Maharishi's face adorned the front covers of many magazines, including *Look, Time, New York Times Magazine* and the *Listener,* journal of the BBC. The prim and spinsterly *Listener* was at pains to make its own position clear in an editorial: "Readers shouldn't fall into the error of supposing that mentioning him and showing his picture means that this journal is a convert to the cause of Transcendental Meditation." The editor wrote himself: "My own view, for what it is worth, is that he is one of the sterling comic figures of the present time."

How did the Maharishi react to comments like these? When he flew into Heathrow from America he said good-humoredly: "These criticisms have no value. What people call me, good or bad, does not matter. I am exposed to millions of views. I cherish them all."

Over 10,000 people flocked to hear his London lectures, but he admitted that most of them went away more puzzled than before. This was almost what Krishnamurti had told me of many of his listeners.

Unlike the great Krishnamurti, however, who stayed privately with friends during his journeys, the Maharishi took rooms at the most lavish hotels—in London he stayed at the Europa, the Hilton and the Waldorf. Asked if this was consistent with the kind of philosophy he was expounding, he merely smiled and said he liked the comfort.

To most ordinary readers of British newspapers Transcendental Meditation was something entirely new and not a little weird. Its impact on youth was enormous and it was consequently somewhat suspect, particularly as young people were at this time showing a disquieting interest in drug-taking and the dubious pleasures of "dropping out," which affronted and disgusted the older generation.

There was a general sigh of relief, therefore, when the Maharishi declared that drugs were not used in his form of religion. Drug addicts, he said, were revealing a weakness of character that was entirely unnecessary. Junkies were searching for something that was not to be condemned but "Transcendental Meditation *is* the something and now I'm here to explain it nobody needs to look through the bottom of a pill bottle."

Drugs had no part in his philosophy and they were, in fact, old hat. Beatle George Harrison said the "truly groovy and trendy source of bliss lay in this new philosophy."

There was, of course, so far as I could see at any rate, nothing at all new in the Maharishi's offerings. Buddhists and Hindus had been using the same system of meditation for thousands of years. What was new was that the whole subject was now in the public eye in the Western hemisphere, it was a matter for public discussion, the techniques were being laid bare for everyone to examine in detail and to adopt, or mock, or respect, or throw out as Oriental eccentricities as they wished.

Theologians joined in the great debate. A pastor in Richmond, Surrey, giving a sermon titled "The Search for Happiness," said the teachings of the Maharishi were scientifically wrong, ineffective in practice and false theologically.

The Reverend Nick Stacey, Rector of Woolwich, took the

opposite view. "Meditation?" he wrote in a newspaper article. "We've practised it for years." Traditionally one form of Christian meditation was to take a passage from scripture, probably an incident in the life of Our Lord, read it and dwell upon it thoughtfully.

"One tries to imagine the scene, one's feelings are stirred, one's understanding of and affection for Christ are increased, which one tries to express in thanksgiving and love. One ends up using one's will to make a resolution which arises out of meditation. For instance if one had been thinking about a story in the Bible which demonstrated Christ's patience with His disciples one might resolve to be more patient with one's own tiresome next door neighbor.

"But there is another form of Christian meditation," Stacey went on, "which appears to have something in common with the transcendental kind and which is becoming increasingly popular with those who try to take their prayers seriously. The theory is simple. Man has a conscious, subconscious and unconscious mind. We think with the conscious mind, the subconscious mind holds many memories which we can easily recall, and the unconscious mind holds memories which we are not able to bring to mind at all.

"Human beings have a tendency to repress unhappy and unpleasant memories, and together with the emotions they stir up, push them down into the unconscious mind. Consequently all of us have fear, resentment, hate and anxiety buried there. This turmoil comes up into the consciousness and is the underlying cause of all sorts of irrational feelings which we do not understand. This can cause terrible unhappiness and even illness.

"In contemplative meditation the aim is to penetrate the unconscious mind with some truth about God which will dissolve the fear and anxieties. It is a way of learning to "wait on" God and in quietness allowing him to make himself known to us. One attempts to relax physically and mentally letting self-concern and self-effort go in order that God may be able to speak to us."

The Reverend Stacey, whom I have not met but whose views I found very relevant, described another method of Christian meditation in which a short sentence, such as "Be still and know that I am peace within you" is repeated over and over. It helps to bypass the conscious mind to allow the truth to sink into the unconscious mind.

"There it will begin to change what is dark and negative. As one perseveres it brings about changes in character. One becomes more peaceful and calm and learns to have a deep love which changes our personal relationship. One begins to experience what Our Lord spoke of as fullness of life."

Quick results were not to be expected; proof of its value, said the rector, came at length in a much deeper awareness of the reality of God. The rector felt, therefore, that the traditional Christian methods of meditation were as helpful as the transcendental kind. "Our problem is not so much not knowing what to do but stirring ourselves out of our lethargy to do it."

What he was describing seemed to me a remarkably close parallel to the Buddhist and Hindu mantra method of meditation.

One result of all this preoccupation with Indian philosophy in the summer and autumn of 1967 was an unprecedented boom in inquiries at the London offices of the Spiritual Regeneration Movement, which had been set up by the Maharishi in 1962. There was also a boom on the materialistic front. India was suddenly "in".

One newspaper reported that an Indiacraft shop in London was completely sold out of plaster and ivory gods. Carnaby Street, center of the trendy clothes industry in London, was enjoying a bonanza with Indian fashions for men. Beatle George Harrison, studying the sitar under the brilliant Ravi Shankar, declared he felt India was his second home.

Nevertheless, behind the secular fringe effect there was a genuine curiosity. Had the Indians got something we hadn't? The influential *London Evening Standard* declared that in the West there had always been a feeling that the East was in closer contact with unspecified mysteries than ourselves. Among the overpoweringly practical societies in the civilized West there was the nagging feeling that somewhere along the line we had lost something. This, in a nutshell, was how I felt too.

The *Evening Standard* added that always when a new religious figure arrived from the East he inspired passionate devotion among his followers. It was certainly true of the Maharishi Mahesh Yogi and he also seemed to inspire something else as well, a kind of indulgent affection among the general public as a whole for they had come to the conclusion that he was not a dangerous influence on their teenage children. If he was not exactly the comic figure which the *Listener* had labelled him, he was definitely humorous and good hearted.

When he finally left London for Holland and more lecture engagements, his farewell at Heathrow airport was as captivating a performance as any he had yet given.

According to one paper the teacher of Transcendental Meditation had omitted to meditate beforehand on the advisability of buying an airline ticket in advance. He bought one and got his luggage weighed just five minutes before his flight was due to leave. Then he couldn't find his passport, "a situation," said the *Daily Mirror*, "which he resolved after a short meditative session."

An anxious BEA girl implored him to hurry, then, thinking he was trotting along behind her, turned to find him distributing flowers among the crowds who had come to see him off. He gave his last, breathless, news conference to the London journalists as he ran across the tarmac to the waiting plane, which eventually left twenty minutes late.

The Maharishi had taken youth by storm. Only a few weeks before his arrival in London Miss Alice Bacon of the Home Office was sadly chiding pop stars for encouraging drug-taking by their impressionable fans. One of the Beatles had given her a dusty answer by publicly commending LSD as an avenue to a full experience of God. Now the Beatles had forsworn drugs, found themselves a guru and turned to the path of Transcendental Meditation.

Commented the *Methodist Recorder*: "The least that can be said is that an Indian mystic is better than cannabis or heroin. There may well be something important in the development, odd though it seems. The rebellion is against the values of aggressive materialism. It is a withdrawal from the rat race. It springs from dissatisfaction with a money-dominated civilization.

"It would undoubtedly be better if the revolt were positive and constructive but it should not be a matter of regret that there is a revolt at all. Perhaps the secular Christians who have been telling us to adapt to secular civilization have missed something that these youngsters want and need. Could it be the note of the eternal in Christian preaching?"

There was considerable speculation on the amount of money poured into the Maharishi's organization by the highly paid show biz personalities who were among his most ardent followers. There had been reports that the Beatles were to build a temple of love in the Himalayas and they planned to go to Rishikesh for a teaching course at the Maharishi's academy. The Maharishi said he would dearly love them to endow a temple but nothing was settled, and in fact as far as I know no more was heard of the project.

It was well-known, however, that serious followers were expected to donate one week's pay to the organization to help spread the teachings. In the case of the Beatles and a few others this would amount to thousands of pounds, but the four young men refused to tell how much, if anything, they had handed over.

What motivated the Beatles to follow Transcendental Meditation? Ringo Starr explained it in one interview like this: "The four of us have had the most hectic lives. We have got almost anything money can buy, but when you can do that the things money can buy mean nothing after a time. You look for something else, for a new experience. We have found something now which fills the gap."

The *London Times* described the Maharishi as the Charles Atlas of spiritual teachers. Just as Charles Atlas' methods did give the persistent enthusiast muscles, those so enthused by the Maharishi might find their way to peace of mind. The Maharishi summed up the problem of the age as spiritual poverty in the midst of material plenty.

The Spiritual Regeneration Movement, the Maharishi's London organization, was first registered in Britain in 1962 as a charitable organization. Its offices are in Grosvenor Place, Westminster. The organization has set up training centers for meditation in fifty countries. I was interested to hear that a spokesman of the movement claimed the big advantage of the Maharishi's philosophy over other types of meditation was that they often demanded sacrifices and the giving up of worldly ways. "This philosophy suits the world as it is."

"Take the Maharishi himself," he said. "He has held press conferences all over the world and rushes from capital city to capital city. This is hectic twentieth-century life, but he's always smooth and calm and humorous. When he replies to questions he is basic and simple, he gives the obvious answers and not the clever-clever ones."

The Maharishi's teaching received praise in that most august of

British institutions, the House of Lords. During a debate on religious teaching in State schools Lord Aberdare told members of the Upper House: "A lot of the time we teach religion the wrong way round. We teach facts and rules and expect our pupils to accept them and lead their lives by them, when what we should draw attention to are their own problems, the problems of life around them and from that draw the religious implications.

"One of the most significant things which has happened has been the conversion of the Beatles to the teachings of the Maharishi Mahesh Yogi. I do not know anything of the teachings of this gentleman but what I do know is that the Beatles have reached the height of worldly achievement and found this not enough. They have sought some spiritual satisfaction."

And so it went on and on. I followed the reports with interest. Hardly a day passed in which there was not some fresh news or comment about the Maharishi's activities, his philosophy or his vast following, mostly of young people eager to find peace, truth, happiness or something which would serve as a spiritual panacea to the complexities, the false values, the day-to-day problems of the world today.

It seemed there was hardly a distinguished public figure who did not enter into the public controversy, not a newspaper which had not expressed its weighty opinion, one way or the other, if only to be in the swim.

When the Beatles finally went to Rishikesh in Northern India the newspapermen went before them. To everyone's surprise reports came in that the Maharishi's neighbors regarded him with almost as much curiosity as the nonmeditating population of England. They were used to Hindu holymen who conducted their lessons in one thatched room; his modern establishment, on the other hand, was known locally as *chourashi kothi*, meaning house with eighty-four rooms.

Around £5,750 had been spent on equipping the colony to standards that would be acceptable to the Westerners who constituted most of the visitors. Even the vegetarian dishes that made up the normal diet were prepared to meet Western tastes. The Maharishi's own five-room residence was equipped with bath and shower and had a fitted kitchen with electric stoves, ovens and hotplates, more in the style of a wealthy business tycoon's retreat than that of a sage or mystic.

The main buildings were in six blocks arranged on a promenade. Each bedroom had its own bathroom with running water, but the beds were simple wood cots and the life of the community ascetic.

Power came from the State's hydroelectric system but the estate had an independent water supply from the mountain streams. The estate had its own printing press and a flour mill to grind wheat.

Locally, the Maharishi was not regarded as a saint or a sage. Some of the more conventional Hindus in the district scorned him as unscientific. His methods included none of the practices such as breath control in which they believed. He never used music or singing in his meditations though he sometimes recited prayers aloud.

Nevertheless, the Maharishi's daily routine was a simple one and seemed to me to conform to tradition. It began early with an hour of meditation and a prayer followed by his discourse to followers who were attending the academy. He ate a simple vegetarian lunch and then took an afternoon nap, after which he began evening classes which were said to occupy him until late at night.

Then the climax came—or I might say the crash. The Beatles, with other celebrities, turned up at Rishikesh for a three-month course in meditation. The academy was heavily guarded and ringed with barbed wire. Within ten days Ringo Starr was back home, saying the food was too spicy and didn't suit him and he and his wife Maureen missed their children. The meditation center? "It was a bit like a holiday camp."

None of Ringo's colleagues stayed the course either, but at least all still spoke highly of the philosophy, if not of its leader, when they returned. "We made a mistake," said one of them. "We thought there was more to him than there was. He's human. We thought at first he wasn't."

The world never found out precisely in what way the Maharishi had shown himself to be human after all, but it was clear he had turned out to be a disappointment. "We're still 100 per cent for meditation, but we're not 100 per cent for the Maharishi," said Ringo. The Maharishi countered this by saying he still loved the Beatles and so long as they went on with their meditation "they needn't come back to me." They had "done very well" at meditation but, because they failed to finish the course, could not be awarded the qualifications to spread his teachings. "We didn't want that anyway," said the Beatles. "It was only a stepping stone in our lives, just like taking LSD was."

The Beatles, disillusioned, went back to work. The sceptics said "I told you so." The Maharishi carried on with his preaching, but when he turned up to lecture at Keele University in North Staffordshire only a handful of his followers welcomed him with adulation and there were no longer the accustomed crowds of fans at the gates.

Then, in June 1968, came his admission of failure. At a press conference in Sydney he said sadly: "I set out in 1960 and gave myself nine years to spread the message around the world, but I know I have failed. I shall retire to a quiet place next year. I have been able to reach a lot of people but my mission is over.

When I visited Rishikesh to find out for myself what had gone wrong I found the gates of the meditation center locked and barred. "The Maharishi is not well," I was told. "He has gone into the hills. He won't see anybody."

❀

For my own part, I did not subscribe to the Maharishi's belief that he had failed. The ballyhoo that had surrounded his mission, the sensational publicity he had received during 1967 and the early part of 1968 and the fatal attraction he seemed to have for entertainers and others for whom success was measured in newspaper column inches were an intolerable distraction and one which, in the end, proved too much for him.

But I could see no reason why he should regard his strenuous and dedicated work over the previous eight years as a flop. I believe his system of meditation is a form of self-hypnosis which in the long run would be rejected as unfulfilling by most people, but at the height of his crusade he certainly succeeded in diverting the attention of many youngsters the world over from the misuse of harmful drugs. He had in fact, achieved a great deal.

I wrote to a friend, Guru Shamar, who ran an institute for the adult blind at Dehradun, a small town on the Ganges near Rishikesh, and told him my wife and I were about to pay him a visit. Shamar replied that he would meet us at New Delhi because, as it happened, he had to pick up a jeep and trailer there at about the time I expected to arrive.

This was handy; the part of the journey I was dreading was the 180-mile train trip in the inevitable crowded, stench-filled train. Shamar met us as arranged and we did the run in just over six hours along the bumpy, dusty road, part tarmac and part cart track that led up into the hills.

We passed through villages of hungry people and in one town where we stopped to fix a flat tire a minor Sikh official tried to prevent me taking photographs. He thought my pictures would be degrading to the villagers which of course was not true; it was an average Indian village with nothing more or less impoverished about it than many others.

We arrived at Dehradun tired, dirty and bruised. Shamar's wife and child greeted us with a display of affection and we were ready for the meal and refreshing drinks that were put before us. Next day Shamar drove us to Rishikesh.

Our first glimpse of the Maharishi's celebrated academy was awe-inspiring. It perched 1,200 feet up in the mighty Himalayas, high above Rishikesh itself which lay reflected in India's holiest of holy rivers, the Ganges. The setting was beautiful. All was peacefulness. So near its source the Ganges—which at Benares and Calcutta was a sluggish, coffee-colored soup, filled with dirt and debris—was here fresh and clean and mountain cold.

Priests and holymen were washing away their sins at its shores and it was not long before Eve and I were following their example, so inviting did the water look. Hundreds of big, fat fish swam about its surface totally unafraid of the humans wading in their midst, as if they knew that vegetarianism was the strict rule in those parts. Sitting in groups talking or moving about together in ones and twos were the countless yogis, priests, sadhus and swamis who, said my friend, found the place so conducive to meditation and learning.

We went into a bookshop and bought some books. There was a drugstore where herbal drugs including marijuana were provided for the villagers and religious followers. At one end of the town a bridge over the Ganges was lined with honourable beggars; strategically placed money changers were there to change our money into fistfuls of small coins so that we would then drop it into the beggar's begging bowls and thereby gain merit.

Shamar introduced us to a swami who with his long hair, beard and robes looked exactly like pictures of Jesus Christ. He had an institute of learning along the river outside the town. The swami took us up to his room which was decorated with extremely beautiful paintings he had made of Buddha and other religious figures.

We were given tea and biscuits and the swami then put on a demonstration of fortune telling. He promised to tell us what was on our minds. He said my wife was interested in having children and was concerned about family matters; I was more interested in business affairs. This did not seem too impressive for women would naturally think about family things and men about business.

He sat down on the floor in the lotus position, the typical Eastern meditative attitude with his legs crossed, and said he would show us how he could control the blood flow to his feet. One foot turned white and the other stayed red—of course one foot was underneath where the veins were constricted while the other was on top folded under. Obviously the blood would flow in one foot and not in the other. But although none of his hokum took us in I had to admit the swami was a very healthy looking and peaceful man and I guess he did derive benefit from his meditation.

He had a collection of cactuses and other thorn plants in which he was very interested. They symbolized his bed of thorns, he told us. I discussed with him the typical Indian methods of meditation, using the *mantra*, but I felt he was not too well versed in the subject. At least I learned nothing new from him.

Rishikesh is the home of the Divine Life Society, and we found the headquarters of this religious organization, which has meditation centers in many countries, on the banks of the river. We noticed a cluster of newspaper reporters and photographers at its doors and with them a small crowd of onlookers. Some of them were foreigners dressed in typical Indian costumes.

There was a buzz of excitement and at first when I approached some of the bystanders, whom I guessed to be Westerners, to find out what was happening, I could get nothing out of them. Whatever it was that was holding their attention they did not seem to want to talk about it. They were distinctly unfriendly.

The Indians proved to be more talkative, however, and we

learned that a luncheon was being given for the society's new leader, Swami Chidananda, who that day was embarking on an overseas tour.

Rishikesh was a haven of peace and the ideal setting for religious devotion. The very atmosphere was holy. The pace of life was steady and unhurried, the air warm and pleasant, the river fresh and clear. Giant crows winged aloft with a graceful, lazy motion and cawed laconically at each other. Children ran about at play and a dog snoozed in the sun. Above towered the slopes of the Himalayas, wooded and mysterious.

Why had the Maharishi Mahesh Yogi's mission failed? I was not yet to discover. We climbed the steep hill up through the trees to the mystic's academy which had enjoyed such immense though short-lived fame. The gate was locked and barred. The only residents were a few attendants and they refused to admit us. They even declined to say more than that he was feeling unwell. He had departed into the hills. He had gone to Kashmir. Or they thought he had. Nobody knew when he would return.

A few days later my hopes were suddenly raised. I had booked seats on an Air India flight to Europe from Delhi. We heard that by coincidence the Maharishi had reserved seats in the same plane, so we explained the situation to the airline authorities and switched to first class in order to make the most of whatever chance occurred to speak to him. Just before the flight we got a call from Air India. The Maharishi had cancelled his plans to go to Europe and would not be on the plane. Our hopes dashed, we switched back to economy class.

I spoke to a number of the Maharishi's lieutenants in Delhi but none of them could give us any information. They evaded my questions. There was only one thing to do. When I arrived in London I would pay a week's wages and sign on for a course with the Spiritual Regeneration Movement.

16

The Golden Silence

WESTERN religious culture is almost wholly concerned with the worshipping of God. The vast majority of church-going people attend service for the purpose of praising the Creator in hymns and seeking the Lord's favour in prayer. In spite of Christ's advice that "the Kingdom of Heaven is within you," the popular belief is that it is somewhere else and that it is only possible to get there after death, by good behavior, sticking to the straight and narrow path of righteousness and regular visits to their particular place of worship once a week while in the land of the living.

It is outside the scope of this account to discuss the merits of this kind of faith, for a full study of Western religious codes did not come within the compass of my search for a quiet mind. Yet it is significant that religion on the plane of "let us pray" and "let us give thanks for…" provides genuine comfort to the millions of devout men and women who follow its teaching.

When I settled in Britain, therefore, I determined to probe at least a few of those areas where the mind and its inner recesses are harnessed in the cause of worship. I spent a little time with a closed order of contemplative Benedictine monks, men who have renounced the day-to-day conventions of so-called civilization and instead devote their lives to total communion with God; I met and talked with Quakers for whom silence really is golden; and I presented myself as a subject at a Spiritualist service with results that were uncanny to say the least.

But first I wanted to tie up the loose ends left by the Maharishi Mahesh Yogi after his sudden disappearance from the Transcendental Meditation scene. This man had, after all, wielded an enormous influence once the newspaper and TV commentators had caught up with him, and his message was meditation, the end product peacefulness and a quiet mind.

When we had settled in a flat near my wife's parents at Maidenhead in Berkshire I contacted the Maharishi's Spiritual Regeneration Movement in London with the intention of signing on in the organization. Eve and I were told of a lecture to be given at Caxton Hall on the benefits of meditation and advised to go along. We did so.

The speakers dealt with a number of subjects, business, politics, housework and so on in which meditation could be a source of strength, and at the end of about an hour people in the audience who were interested in taking a course were told to stay on and fill out various membership forms. We stayed behind, took the forms and signed.

A week or so later we received a letter asking us to appear at a house in Kensington where we would be initiated into the movement. We were asked to take along a basket of fruit and a bunch of flowers to act as symbols of respect and giving. At the prescribed time we presented ourselves at the house with our offerings of fruit and flowers and went through the initiation ceremony in which officials of the movement performed round a small altar with candles and incense burning.

The ceremony was a simple affair conducted in a small room on an upper floor. There was no furniture except the altar with candles and a few flowers and one solitary chair. Each individual (there were about five of us) was initiated separately and I went in first while Eve waited downstairs. I was motioned to the chair and sat down

The initiator, a Pole, stood in front of me performing intricate gestures with his hands over the altar and over my head, chanting all the time in Sanskrit. Following the Hindu practice he gave me a mantra word to repeat, going to considerable lengths to demonstrate the correct way to pronounce it and listening to me until I had it off pat.

The word, he told me, had been specially chosen to be appropriate to my personality and character and must not be divulged. Afterwards, Eve and I compared notes (I know, we cheated) and found we had been given the same mantra.

After initiation we were told to go down to the living room in the basement of the house and meditate for half an hour using the mantra, then report back on the results. The process of meditation by means of mantra, as I have already described, involves the repetition of the selected word over and over again. As thoughts enter your mind they are replaced by the mantra until gradually all thinking is eliminated and a mental state of quiet serenity is achieved.

To be fair, I did find the experience fairly effective; it was extremely relaxing both physically and mentally after a while and "spiritual regeneration" was probably a reasonable description of the state produced.

The next stage was our introduction to checkers, experienced meditators whose role was to guide or correct the newcomers in their meditations. I was told to confide in my checker any problems that arose; he would put me right if I was going wrong. My checker told me that as the initiate develops his ability to meditate the point is reached where it is possible to go into a state of deep silence almost spontaneously and without any elaborate preparation.

So long as I made the effort and practised meditation conscientiously for thirty minutes morning and night, as time went by my efficiency would improve and the results would become more and more beneficial. Transcendental Meditation, I was assured, was a natural technique by which anyone could make use of the full capacity of the mind which would result in clear thinking and efficiency in all spheres of living.

Before we left the center we were told that initiates were expected to subscribe the equivalent of a week's wages to the movement. As husband and wife we would be regarded as one individual, however, and one week's pay would be accepted for us both. As it happened we had just arrived in Britain, I had retired from the Secret Service and was still out of work; Eve didn't have a job and so in the end we parted with very little for the privilege of initiation into the Maharishi's mysteries.

I was impressed, as I invariably was when I investigated some new religious area, by the sincerity of everyone I met at the Spiritual Regeneration Movement's center in London. The man who conducted my initiation and my wife's was a peaceful and pleasant person and one who obviously benefited from the practices he preached.

A little while later I struck up a friendship with a London journalist and we visited Marlow in Buckinghamshire where four short talks were to be given by members of the International Meditation Society, which so far as I could gather, was a related concern. Here again, the speakers were cheerful, friendly and peaceful people, three women and a young man, who were so relaxed before their not wholly sympathetic audience that what they had to say was utterly convincing.

Their particular angles were the benefits of Transcendental Meditation upon health, success in life, improved relations with other people and, embracing a somewhat wider field, world peace. They tried manfully (even the ladies) to stick to their respective subjects but it was soon clear that their enthusiasm was getting the better of them and at length each speaker abandoned his notes and spoke with impressive vigor—and what I took to be sheer joy or a good imitation of it—on the benefits of meditation in general rather than specific terms.

And much of what they said made undeniable sense. To lead a good and useful life calls for mental, physical and emotional health. With meditation a regular habit, anxieties and tensions are removed. Make the entire potential of the mind available and your thoughts will be correspondingly more efficient and creative, which in turn will lead to increased achievement without wasted effort. Inner calm will make for more natural relations with the people you meet. Happiness is infectious and a person full of joy will influence everyone he meets.

There was nothing wrong with any of these concepts. World peace? The tensions in the world were the sum of the individual tensions of all people, said the speaker. These tensions were increasing and could, if allowed to go unchecked, cause further wars. The only sure way of tackling the problem was to cool the tensions of the individual. One person meditating could contribute towards world peace and if everyone practised meditation all war could cease.

All the speakers clearly and honestly felt they had a good solution to offer to life's headaches.

❀

Then there were the Quakers. I had heard that Quaker group meditation was a variety of meditation in which the emphasis was on group rather than individual experience and I wanted to find out more.

I spotted an advertisement in a local newspaper announcing a meeting of the Religious Society of Friends at a town just outside London and scheduled for a Sunday morning. I laid aside my Sunday newspaper and set out to find the meeting hall. It was a single story building of fairly common place architecture with little about it of an ecclesiastical nature.

A handwritten notice outside the double doors duplicated what I had read in the newspaper announcement and expressed a welcome to all who wished to come inside.

I pushed open one of the doors and entered. It was a minute or two before the appointed time for the start of the meeting and a few early arrivals were already there. Two rows of chairs were arranged round the perimeter of the small room and out of about twenty half of them were occupied.

There was complete silence. I sat down with the others and looked around. Except for the chairs and a small cabinet containing books and leaflets the room was bare. There was no altar, there were no pictures on the walls, statues or candles, and apparently no minister, priest or group leader in charge of the meeting.

If I expected someone to announce the start of the meeting I was in for a surprise for it soon became clear that it had begun. The meeting was already in session and the silence was part of it. As the minutes ticked by I found myself merging into it; I felt I was sharing with this handful of strangers a kind of spiritual experience which was releasing me from individuality.

About ten minutes had passed, during which the silence continued unbroken in the small room, when a woman suddenly stood up and began talking. She was small, neatly dressed in a light brown coat and brown shoes, and had a pale, earnest face. She spoke quietly but firmly and told the gathering about a personal problem which was affecting her home life.

She described the trouble in detail and said she wished to share with her friends the insight she had gained from it. The meeting listened passively and with an occasional sympathetic glance at the speaker, but without registering any sign of shock or other emotion as the story unfolded. The woman then opened a slim book of Keats' poems and read two or three extracts which applied to the situation. Then she sat down and the silence resumed.

Again the minutes ticked by. A kind of silent communion seemed to exist between the members of the group. Outside a bird whistled and I could see the leaves falling from the trees. The sky was grey. Within the room the only sound came from a silver-haired gentleman whose breathing was heavy.

Then, without any warning, a man in a neat blue striped suit rose to his feet. From the Bible in his hands he read a few verses and proceeded to give his own interpretation of their meaning and their application to present-day life. The other people heard him out, some of them indicating agreement with a slight nod, the rest merely listening passively until he sat down as unobtrusively as he had stood up.

All was silence once more. Then a youngish woman, rather prim, with a pocket-sized Bible in her gloved hand, got up out of her seat and addressed her friends in a low voice on some Christian principles and their relevance to daily problems. Everyone listened in respectful silence. Eventually she too sat down again.

There followed a long silence while I waited for the next speaker to get up. Ten to fifteen minutes passed and I closed my eyes in meditation. The only sound was the old man's breathing. There was no tension in the room as we sat there. There was relaxation. There was a kind of blessed accord among the individuals who were somehow withdrawn within themselves and yet in a state of silent commune with each other.

Suddenly there was the sound of shuffling feet and the scrape of chairs and I opened my eyes. The meeting had reached its conclusion and the people were standing ready to disperse. I rose to leave but as I reached the door a voice behind me said, "Excuse me, is this your first time here?" I turned and found the speaker to be a smiling, middle-aged woman with grey bobbed hair and gold-rimmed glasses.

"Yes," I said. She appeared to be an elder of the congregation. "I'm interested in meditation and thought I'd come along to a Quaker meeting to see how they went about it. I came here because of your notice in the local paper."

She seemed pleased. "I hope you were impressed," she said with a smile. "We really do derive great benefit and peace of mind from our silent devotions." I believed her. The participants in this morning's service were genuine, ordinary people. They had put on their best clothes for the occasion, joined together in silent prayer and spoken, those who wanted to, spontaneously and without embarrassment about experiences which they felt had a certain value that ought to be shared. And then they had gone away refreshed. I had noticed they were all older people with the exception of one young girl about 18, though this may have had no significance. I was impressed.

"Can you tell me more about Quakerism?" I asked. The woman went over to the cabinet and selected several leaflets and a small book which she handed to me. They would give me an introduction to the faith, she said, but meanwhile if there were any questions… The room was now empty except for the two of us and we sat down and had a long discussion.

"To us Quakers," she said, "creeds, rituals, sacred books, sacramentals, priesthood and religious institutions are nothing without the inner experience of the presence of God.

"Our group meditation can be likened to many candles burning in one place, the light from each augmenting the others. So when many are gathered together in the same mental state they become a shining glory to God to the refreshment of each person present."

The woman told me that for three hundred years the Quakers had been meeting in silence without any prearranged program. Each member comes in a receptive mood, neither prepared to speak nor intending not to speak, but with the aim of quieting the mind of daily matters and reaching the center.

"From this sharing of speech and silence do you find something that links the group in an active and creative union with God?" I asked.

"Sometimes the speech of one person sparks off the thoughts of another who expands on the theme and there develops an understanding of a theme larger than the individual," the woman replied.

Intellectual meditation is not the object of the meetings; instead they have as their goal the feeling of the presence of, and unity with,

God. The Quakers believe that out of the love generated from their meetings comes a compassion for the woes of the less fortunate. They feel that faith and deeds are inseparable and voluntarily join in the activities of various social, cultural, religious, professional and political groups with the object to serve.

The woman told me how a Quaker business meeting is conducted. Held each month, they begin in silence and silence is the main feature; there are no arguments, no motions, no secondings, no votes, vetoes or majority decisions. The clerk introduces items of business and if a disagreement seems to be brewing the meeting seeks unity in silence. If disagreement continues the matter is postponed until the next meeting. If agreement is reached on a certain topic it is incorporated into the group.

I couldn't help reflecting on the consequences of such a procedure if the United Nations, Parliament or Congress conducted their business in the fashion of a Quaker business meeting. Progress would be somewhat slower without the customary cut and thrust of debate—though tempers would stay cooler.

I left the Quaker meeting hall with a humble respect for people who have found a harmonious application of silence for coping with real present day problems of society.

Spiritualism is a faith that demands more than a passing mention in this review of Christian practices into which my search led me in Britain. The foundations of Spiritualism are based on the Christian belief in the immortality and survival of the soul, life after death and the existence of a benevolent and omnipotent God. The inevitability of death and the belief in immortality play an important role in the Spiritualists' religious practices.

But my first encounter with the faith was unsatisfactory. Noticing a local newspaper announcement of a service I presented myself at the place of worship at the stated time and joined in the action as a member of the congregation. We started by singing a few hymns which were followed by prayers spoken by the leaders of the group. After a further hymn a clairvoyant was introduced. He was a man of middle years, dressed in a grey tweed suit. Seated in the center of the room in front of the congregation, he purported to relay messages to selected people present from their relatives or acquaintances in the next world.

His particular procedure was to pick out a member of the congregation and concentrate his efforts on that person. The clairvoyant entered into a trance and when "transmissions" began he seemed to me to seek the aid of the subject in delivering the message. "Do you know someone whose name begins with S...or D?"

"No..." said the subject uncertainly.

"Or W?"

"There was a Wilfred who kept the cake shop down the street. He died."

"Yes, Wilfred, Wilfred..." said the clairvoyant, evidently encouraged. "I have a message from Wilfred."

With another subject the clairvoyant, clearly in contact with the next world exclaimed with enthusiasm "Bert...Bert, does the name Bert mean anything to you?"

"No," said the subject.

"Winifred?"

"Yes," said the subject after a pause. "I did know a Winifred who is now in the spirit world. She was a neighbor."

"Well, Winifred is sending you a message," said the clairvoyant. Then after a pregnant pause, "She says that although things are going badly for you on the material plane at the present, they will improve by Christmas and you are to bear with events until then."

I wasn't at all impressed with the performance. This so-called clairvoyant appeared to be playing a guessing game with an occasional correct guess and plenty of mistakes which would easily be corrected by judicious questioning of the subject. His messages always began with a near miss which was then adjusted by the willing subject so that, by degrees, something approaching a plausible story was arrived at.

There were a couple of women for whom he established a fairly convincing communication with departed friends, but I found out later that these women were workers at the church and that the clairvoyant had personal knowledge of their circumstances, which doubtless contributed to the greater accuracy of his contact with their dear ones.

I learned that on Wednesday evenings the church conducted healing services and decided to investigate these procedures which I guessed had more than a little to do with the mind.

An assortment of people attended the services with an assortment of illnesses and complaints in need of treatment. The healers wore long white coats and performed the healing ritual in the center of the hall.

The patient sat on a chair and the healer, after washing his hands, seemed to attune himself with the spiritual plane. When supernatural contact was established the healer placed his hands on the afflicted area of the patient's body to radiate the healing vibrations from the spirit world.

I do not know if these methods were effective but no doubt the element of faith and devotion for the healing power of God provided the sick with some relief.

Further inquiry led me to another Spiritualist church where I would probably be able to witness a better quality of service and watch better clairvoyants in action. This time the experience was more rewarding.

On the occasion I visited this particular church the medium was a woman who seemed to come from a humble background. She established herself in the trance state after selecting a member of the congregation as her subject and proceeded to make contact with this person's loved ones in the spirit world with results that, to me, were nothing short of uncanny in their accuracy.

Her performance was much more impressive than the previous demonstrations I had seen. Not only did she discover the first name of dead relatives through her contact in the spirit world but also their surnames. She mentioned that one subject's mother, now dead, had been fond of a certain type of house plant and that these plants were her favorite pastime while she was alive. The subject confirmed this. The medium mentioned a black cocker spaniel to one subject. Its name was Prince. The subject confirmed that as a child she had had a black cocker spaniel named Prince.

Then I asked to be used as a subject. I was unknown to the people gathered in the room and there could be no chance of their taking me for a ride. The medium lapsed into a trance, eyes closed, body motionless. There was no sound in the room. "I'm getting a call from a man named Sency." I nearly fell off my chair in astonishment. The name was very well known to me; it was the surname of a branch of my family in the United States. The medium mentioned a Christian name; it was that of a dead uncle on my father's side.

"This person has a message for you," said the clairvoyant. I was listening with intense interest now. The situation was unreal. Uncle John had lived some distance from my home and I had seen little of him in the last few years before he died. What possible reason could he have for wishing the communicate with me from wherever he was now?

"There is a message for you," repeated the medium. I waited. "He mentions a letter...there is a letter coming to you...soon...in the next two days...." There was a pause and the medium seemed to be trying to understand something.

"The letter will cause you to take a long journey...journey over the sea...you will remain overseas for about twelve months before returning to England...."

End of message. If I wanted to invent a communication from a dead relative I think I could have done a lot better than that. The letter, the sea journey, these were the ingredients used by fairground fortune tellers since the beginning of time, or since fortune tellers began. All that was missing was that as a result of my journey I would become rich.

But this "fortune teller" had mentioned the source of the information, an uncle with whom I had not been very close and whose name, in any case, had certainly not passed my lips during the time I had been in England.

And another factor with which the medium was definitely not acquainted was that some weeks previously I had applied for a job in the United States.

The position, if I got it, would involve the control of security arrangements for a big North American company which was the kind of work I'm equipped to do with the training and background I have, but to date I had heard nothing since attending a personal interview in London.

Yet another factor was that the proposed contract was for a period of twelve months so it was my intention to live in the States for twelve months and then return to Britain.

It all fit, yet the clairvoyant could have known none of these circumstances.

Even more remarkable was the fact that two days later I received a letter from the company offering me the job. The same evening my phone rang and the operator said there was a call on the line from the States. Terms of employment were agreed there and then and I was asked to leave for New York as soon as possible.

That was two days after my visit to the Spiritualist church and my selection as a subject for the clairvoyant. In other words, at the time of my encounter with the medium the letter was already on its way. Presumably the company's board knew about it, so would the typist who typed it, but how did Uncle John know? And a clairvoyant in a small Spiritualist church in the Home Counties?

After this Spiritualist service I stayed behind to buttonhole one of the church leaders. I wanted to find out a little more about the principles of the religion and its strange and supernatural powers. The minister I approached seemed very willing to impart whatever information I needed and, as in the Quaker meeting hall, we sat down in a couple of seats for a discussion.

"Your services seem to consist almost entirely of communication sessions with dead spirits," I began. "What sort of people are the clairvoyants who conduct these sessions?"

"Mediums are certain sensitive individuals who have a highly clairvoyant ability. While in a trance they are able to receive messages from spirits—not dead spirits, please—who are anxious to reach and communicate with relatives or friends still on earth. They are able to give information which frequently is known only by the deceased person and which could not be obtained by normal means," he said. "Such statements are confirmed or denied by the relative or friend in question."

"How does Spiritualist healing work—and does it work?' I asked, fearing my informant might be hurt by the unintentional emphasis which undoubtedly betrayed my scepticism. "What are the techniques used?"

"Of course it works," he replied. "The Divine spirit in man is inexhaustible and perfect. It is continually expressing itself. One only has to believe in it for it to manifest itself. To recognize the Divine principle in action is the fundamental principle underlying

Spiritualist healing. The healers have an intimate knowledge of this subject and thereby have acquired the power to heal.

"You see, afflictions have been brought on by man himself and not by God, and therefore the application of spiritual and natural laws bring about a cure. The power to heal lies dormant in all of us but it is highly awakened and developed in the healers of the Spiritualist church.

"As to actual technique, the healing power of the spiritual forces passes from the healer to the patient in the form of vibrations, a kind of magnetic flow. The healer is a medium through which the spiritual healing power flows on the physical plane through the hands, the eyes and the mind of the healer and into the afflicted part of the patient's body.

"It is important for the healer to induce the patient to relax absolutely," he went on. "Only in a truly relaxed condition can a patient become properly attuned to the emanating flow of healing powers. A feeling of warmth is frequently felt by the patient in the area of trouble as he feels the transference of healing vibrations from the medium. Blood circulation rate increases and mind and body become harmonious.

The patient is told that the power to cure lies within himself and when this is appreciated fully the spiritual energy released from within brings with it a tremendous feeling of relief. A cure will usually follow. In cases where a patient is treated through the nervous system excessive amounts of nerve energy are created in the body and these, together with the healing power of the medium, cause large flows of blood to the critical area thus the body's natural eliminative and nutritional processes are activated. Again, a cure soon takes place and full health is restored.

My informant introduced other Spiritualists, including a healer, to me during our conversation and they added their contribution to the sum of knowledge I gained about this strange and unconventional branch of the Christian religion, which brought into play the human mind as an essential piece of spiritual equipment. I thanked the people I had met for so enthusiastically and generously imparting information and left with a clearer understanding of the controversial subject of Spiritualism.

✸

Shortly after my wife and I arrived in Britain we were invited to have tea one afternoon with an old friend of hers who lived at Burnham in Buckinghamshire. From the window of her sitting room we could see a large white building across the street and I asked her what it was.

"That's the monastery, Nashdom Abbey," she replied. "Benedictine monks. They're a contemplative society and really we see very little of them." I tried to press her for more information but without success. From her vantage point so close to the monastery walls she saw hardly anything of the inhabitants and knew even less about their activities, other than the fact that some of the food grown within the monastery grounds was sold at a shop in the village. I made a mental note to investigate later, and when, a short time afterwards, I found myself in Burnham once more I decided to pay the brothers a call.

I parked the car near what I took to be the main entrance and rang the doorbell. There was no response and I kept on ringing. Still there was no answer and I was wondering what my next move should be when a car drew up outside another part of the building. The driver got out and entered the monastery through a door in the wall, so I decided to follow suit. The door led to a reception hall containing a few stands on which was stacked reading material concerning the Benedictine order. It was obviously meant to be taken by anyone interested and I help myself to two or three pamphlets. The sound of voices was coming from a room to my right and, on investigation, I found myself in a large chapel where monks, dressed in dark gowns, were attending mass.

Not wishing to disturb them at their devotions I quietly closed the chapel door and left the reception hall by another door which led outside to a beautifully kept garden. Thinking that mass would be over soon I sat down on the grass to browse through the papers I had picked up until someone came along to whom I could talk. I didn't have to wait long. The monks filed out of the chapel in silence a few minutes later and moved off in various directions.

I stopped one and asked where I could get some information about the life of the monastery and the activities of the brothers. "Wait here," he said. "I will send Dom Joseph to speak to you. He's the guest master and he will attend to your inquiries."

Dom Joseph was extremely helpful. Tall, in his early fifties, with scarcely any color in his drawn cheeks and not much of his grey hair left, he told me the monastery did not go out of its way to encourage guests but it did provide guest rooms for those who wished to visit and spend a quiet period in rest and religious practice.

I told him I was interested to know more about the monastic life of the Benedictines and their contemplative practices and would very much like to accept his offer to stay for a few days at Nashdom Abbey. We set a date for the following week.

As I drove home I wondered how I was going to break the news to Eve that I was about to pack a bag and leave her. But I have a very understanding wife and when the moment came to explain what I had in mind it was not difficult. After all, I would be away for less than a week—and not more than a few miles away at that—and after almost a year of married life I felt she would be quite glad to have me out of the house for a bit. It would be a pleasant change from having me turning up for meals regularly and would be in fact a rest for her as much as for me. So I did not lose sight of the value for both of us in my proposed trip to Nashdom.

I packed a few clothes in a small grip with some books and my writing materials, gave Eve a kiss and drove off. Dom Joseph was expecting me. He showed me to my room which was in the gatehouse of the abbey. It was small, neat and clean, furnished with a few pieces of essential furniture of ancient vintage including a desk and chair. I was given a schedule for meals and shown where the dining room was located, and then invited to attend mass after I had settled in. I went to mass and afterwards joined the monks in a half hour of prayer and silent meditation, during which they sat completely still with their heads bowed.

Next day, after I had breakfasted simply, a visitor called at my room and introduced himself as Dom John. He said he was going to attempt to give me a little background information on the Benedictine order and outline the purposes and routine of monastic life. We took a walk out into the sunshine and he led me out of the abbey grounds over fields and meadows, which were part of the abbey property, and up a hill to the beautiful flower garden of their nearest neighbor who Dom John told me was a wealthy newspaper magnate.

We stopped from time to time to admire the beauty of the

surrounding countryside and I felt that if anyone should really want to retreat from the hurly-burly of modern business life and seek perpetual peace and quiet this was surely a good place to try it. Just then a Boeing 707 dropped low over the hill on its way to Heathrow and shattered the stillness with its roar.

"We follow the rules which St. Benedict laid down to govern the lives of monks," he told me. "Benedict was a puritan of the sixth century. But we don't interpret his rules as strictly or as puritanically as some do. The Trappists, for instance, are strict vegetarians and they don't use speech for communicating at all; they employ a sign language like the deaf-and-dumb. We regard it as Christian charity to speak to guests.

"And one day every month we can put on ordinary clothes and go out into the world, return to our families if we want to. That, too, gives us spiritual refreshment." Each of the monks held a position in the monastery which contributed to the running, maintenance and administration of the place. "All of us, except the elderly and senior administrators, help out on a rotating basis with the menial jobs about the place, such as sewing, mending, preparing the food and cooking it, and taking care of the garden.

"As you have already seen we have well organized gardens and greenhouses. We grow all our own vegetables. Our day starts before dawn and goes on until well after sunset. We spend the morning in prayer and go about our assigned duties in the afternoon.

"All the monks here expect to go to heaven. The purpose of our monastic life with its strictness and its physical severity is quite simply personal sanctification but our wish to become saints is not motivated by dreams of self-glory; it's that we want to be able to intercede with God on behalf of mankind. Monasticism is opposed to the materialistic way of life outside and temptation and weakness are checked by keeping out of its path to a great extent."

"You must feel at times that you're losing contact with the outside world," I suggested.

"Not at all," said Dom John. "If we lose contact it is because we want to, but in fact we maintain contact very well in comparison with some orders. We meet our visitors, people like yourself who come here for spiritual reasons and sometimes take a walk into the village."

The monks vow themselves to poverty, chastity and obedience. The abbey at Burnham is largely self-supporting, incense is manufactured there for sale to various churches but little real revenue is needed. The men till their own soil, make their own clothes. I noticed that part of the abbey building was fairly new and asked Dom John if this was because extra living space was needed owing to an increase in the number of people turning to the monastic way of life.

"The new wing is to be used for the training of novices," he said. "Not all novices stay long enough to take their final vows, of course. The demands upon one are very exacting. The life is hard. And although we train many new monks we also lose monks because they become unhappy here or want to get married."

Life certainly was austere for me during the week I spent at the abbey. The food, although no doubt nourishing, was simple and basic. The one luxury the monks allowed themselves was to listen to classical music or perhaps Gilbert and Sullivan on a homemade hi-fi set on Sunday afternoons. Otherwise the life was totally uneventful. A library stocked with thousands of religious works was another source of relief from the monotonous routine. Books by St. John of the Cross, St. Theresa and the Trappist Thomas Merton helped me to while away the long hours and served to fill me in on the values of a contemplative life. One of the books from the library was always taken to the dining hall at meal times and while the others ate in silence one of the brothers read passages aloud out of the book.

But I had come to Nashdom Abbey with my interest in meditation very much in mind. I asked the abbot what happened during the half-hour of silence which followed the evening service every day. "Most of us spend that time contemplating a passage from the Scriptures or from other religious work," he answered.

"What are your views on the Maharishi's approach to religion?" I asked. The abbot smiled.

"We feel an essential of true spiritual life is suffering, as demonstrated by Christ's suffering on the Cross for mankind. The Maharishi says suffering is unnecessary and he sees no reason for it. There we differ. But the brother of one of our monks was a follower of the Maharishi and he gained tremendous benefit from meditation."

"Would you permit one of your monks to take a course of meditation from the Maharishi?" I asked.

"I should have to select the candidate very carefully if it was ever considered," he said.

❁

Although I was born and raised in the Christian faith my knowledge of Eastern religious cultures was far more extensive. After spending five days at Nashdom Abbey in the company of its devout Benedictine monks and living their austere and comfortless life, reading their religious books, enjoying their beautiful environment, suffering their dull routine, I felt I knew a little more about its meaning.

But still there was something missing. I had glimpsed the strange phenomena of faith healing and communication with the dead in a Spiritualist church. I had sunk with my Quaker friends into a rich contemplative silence. I had reaped the rewards of a brief encounter with monasticism, but something was missing still. I had seen faith, joined in prayer, shared silence, even chanted the Hindu mantra in a Kensington basement with some result, but there was still confusion and turmoil. What was missing was a quiet mind, the whole object of my search.

My thoughts went back to Rangoon and the hilltop meditation center of the remarkable U Ba Khin. There I knew I had come close to finding what I was looking for. I began to see that sooner or later I would have to go back.

17

Three Wise Men: the Search is Over

IT was clearly time I took stock of the situation. My researches had led me along many strange paths and the time had come for me to distinguish somehow between the dead-ends and those which might bring me nearer to my goal.

There was much that I'd seen and heard which had to be rejected as irrelevant pop-religious trash and, of course, much to respect which, while doing nothing for me, nevertheless commanded devout followings of sincere and intelligent people.

On the other hand I knew that a few luminaries, and only a few, did possess the kind of insight or enlightenment for which I yearned.

There was a lot to be learned, for instance, from Suzuki, U Ba Khin and Krishnamurti, the three men in the world who, for me, held the elusive secret of mind quietude. But the great Suzuki was now dead. Krishnamurti roamed the world and had no permanent resting place; meetings with him had to be largely a matter of chance. I had not, at this time come to hear of Brockwood, the center of Krishnamurti's work which was being set up in the beautiful Hampshire countryside. And U Ba Khin was resident in faraway Burma, a land where foreigners are not exactly made to feel welcome.

I read and reread the notes I had made following my meeting with Suzuki, that erudite twentieth-century wise old man of Zen, and pored over his published works. I played back, over and over, my Krishnamurti tapes and reexamined the words that had spilled from his lips during our conversations; and the advice he had given me. I was a young man feeding on the fruits of an old man's lifetime of enlightenment and experience; here was a saint, perhaps, and a pundit, a scholar and an ordinary fellow, relaxed, brimful of health in mind and body. He had what I was looking for all right.

And there was U Ba Khin, the beaming globe-faced *guruji* who had so clearly shown me that the light of nirvana was shaded by no obstruction so impenetrable as my own busy and mischievous mind. Here, also, was a truly powerful source of inspiration in spite of all the thousands of miles that now lay between us.

To be truthful, I had become thoroughly discouraged with the negative results of my search for a quiet mind. I had probed so many areas where a positive answer should have been forthcoming and met only with failure, or at most a dim glimmer of understanding. In the months that followed my inquiries at Nashdom Abbey I became overwhelmed with melancholy. I was disappointed to the very brink of despair with my experiences of what man had done with Buddha's light. Despite all I'd seen, heard and experienced in the months and years since the spark had first ignited in me, just where had it got me? Nowhere. Or almost nowhere.

And yet I felt intuitively the search was moving towards a climax of some sort. I had accumulated as firm a groundwork and served as exhaustive an apprenticeship as any Westerner could hope for in the mysteries of the East; my mind was ready for the supreme experience which continued to elude me. The question was, could I make it or would my entire mission end in failure? I felt the target was now within reach; would I miss the bull's eye by inches but miss it just the same?

The closest I had come to the transcending of my devilish mind was at the meditation center in Rangoon and I had kept in touch from time to time with U Ba Khin. The old man was predictably horrified when he heard about my visit to a Christian monastery for a period of Buddhist meditation. Surely there would be a conflict of forces, he wrote.

"In the days of Buddha," he said in a letter, "a monk by the name of Meghiya was accompanying Buddha on his return from the morning round of alms. When they reached a beautiful spot by the side of a riverine with nice trees to give shade Meghiya suggested to Buddha that it looked a good place for meditation. He asked to be allowed to stay at the spot to meditate for the rest of the day. Buddha knew that the place was infested with spiritual forces of the lower order not amenable to Buddha-Dhamma so he told Meghiya the place was not appropriate for the purpose. But when Meghiya was very eager to take his chance Buddha kept quiet.

"After a time Meghiya returned to the monastery unable to make any progress in meditation although the place had seemed to be all right. Appearances are deceptive. Meghiya had all the time at his disposal in his capacity as a monk for religious work. But you have very little time and out of that very little time I do not want you to take chances and waste the precious time."

I knew I deserved the sage's mild ticking off but I didn't take it too much to heart; I felt justified in pursuing my inquiries wherever there was a promising lead and, indeed, had I not followed this broad-minded policy it is doubtful whether I would have encountered U Ba Khin himself and his meditation center in Burma.

But I felt increasingly drawn to return there. All my intellectual arousing had me so frustrated that I felt I had reached the point where I must give up the speculative search and approach the situation with an open, receiving mind rather than with preconceived ideas of how I was going to bring on the purifying and cleansing transcendental state. After all, I had already been taught to realize that you do not go after it, it comes to you when the search stops.

I put away all my notebooks, pencils and papers and tape recorder and prepared myself to let come what may. I assumed an attitude of neutrality, neither enthusiastic for success nor anxious about possible failure. I placed myself at the mercy of providence. "Not my will, Lord, but thine be done in me and through me." I had difficulty obtaining visas for myself and my wife to enter Burma but in the end we were successful.

We arrived at Rangoon airport at sunset on the Buddhist New Year and the whole population seemed to be joining in the celebrations. We were met by two members of the meditation center staff who drove us through streets which were wild with gaiety. The Buddhist New Year, like our own, is an occasion for going a little mad and thousands of people lined the streets dressed in their traditional longyi, all soaking wet. It's the custom to throw buckets of water over each other as a symbol of washing one's friends' sins away although, on a more practical level, the tradition also serves to cool off the excited multitudes dancing and shouting in the tropical heat.

Our driver cautioned us to keep the car windows turned up,

otherwise we risked a severe soaking. Realizing we were foreigners, the crowds of natives took great delight in seeing that we actively participated in the festivities. For a while we followed our driver's advice but the heat inside the car was stifling and the sweat pouring from our bodies was as drenching as any festive water thrown in fun by the delirious Burmese and at last we could keep the windows shut no longer.

In came the water with a rush and in no time at all we were dripping from head to foot. Eve was hooting with laughter and the coolness of the water was much easier to bear, despite the discomfort, than the choking heat had been. But Eve didn't spot where some of the water came from, out of the open streams which also served as drains along the side of the road. I'm sure if she'd realized what some of the contents of those streams were she would not have been quite so amused by the whole business. But it didn't take me long to adopt a philosophical attitude to the affair and we made our tortuous way towards the meditation center suffering the lesser of the two evils.

But progress was slow. The fever of the New Year celebrations was at its peak and the sheer spectacle and color were a marvel to our Western eyes. It was Eve's first visit to Rangoon and our genial driver insisted on taking us the long way round so that we could see as many of the sights as possible. Perhaps the most remarkable were the huge garishly painted floats parading in the main streets in competition for the festival prizes. The crowds were whooping with delight as each new float appeared and made its way along the street. Men, women and children were shrieking with hysterical joy, splashing about in their soaked clothes and embracing each other in a wild, intoxicating demonstration of good cheer. The weird strains of musical instruments mingled with the laughing and shouting and the din made our heads spin.

At last we left the noise and spectacle behind us and made for U Ba Khin's meditation center. By the time we arrived night had fallen and there was blackness everywhere. We were greeted by some of the smiling friends who recognized me from my previous visit and they escorted us to the main hall where U Ba Khin lectures to those who come to hear him. I greeted him in the traditional Burmese style by kneeling on the floor and bowing three times, touching my head on the floor in front of his feet. I had remembered to bring a few orchid plants for his garden for I knew these were his favorite flower. His face, with its round, ample cheeks, was wreathed in smiles.

"It's a great pleasure to see you again, Coleman," he said. I returned the compliment and said it was good to be back. I introduced Eve and he asked her if she had enjoyed seeing a little of their New Year festivities. "Tonight we hold a special New Year service. You must come and join us if you wish."

We were standing there dripping from top to toe and small pools of water were forming beneath our feet. We were glad to be shown to our rooms and quickly washed away the grime of the journey and changed into dry things. I looked forward to a long conversation with the master but when we emerged from our quarters a sumptuous meal was laid for us in the dining room. It was past midnight before I had a chance to talk. The question arose whether the goal of nirvana was a selfish one. I had to admit it was. U Ba Khin was very concerned that it should not remain so but rather be put to use in helping others.

"All actions must have a beginning and true compassion originates not as a philosophical ideal but as a feeling which motivates us to help others," he said. I was to find out later that the goal of nirvana, while originating in the somewhat selfish desire for a quiet mind, is in fact experienced as a very wholesome and rewarding state; a fine point is reached where there is a gentle slipping over to a state free from desire. Akin to the question of a "selfish" search for nirvana— the seeking of a quiet mind which, if acquired, would be a benefit to oneself—was the possibility that my search was a form of escapism. I felt pretty sure that in my case it was nothing of the sort but U Ba Khin showed me that the possibility had to be faced.

"In Buddhism one is not escaping socially acquired guilts or senses of duty which are dictated by social mores. Instead one is entrusted with the energy and efficiency in which compassion and spontaneity compel us to help others," he said.

I realized I would have to take a fresh look at my motives. I was certain I was not trying to escape from anything: my life was proceeding along fairly sound and satisfying lines, I'd had my share of thrills and spills and now I was enjoying the prospect of settling down with my lovely wife and raising a family of young Colemans. The future looked good. What should I need to escape from?

But inasmuch as I had seen the benefits of the "quiet mind"

state in others it was not out of the question that I sought it for myself from motives of self-satisfaction. U Ba Khin was now adding another dimension, a dimension which he had amply demonstrated and exemplified in his own life.

But if I was to get down to serious business there was no time like the present and although it was very late I decided to finish the day with a spot of meditation in a small room in the pagoda which I'd got to know so well during my previous visits.

International Meditation Centre, Rangoon, Burma

While my talk with U Ba Khin was proceeding Eve had been finding her way around the center and meeting some of the other visitors. She was now in bed and asleep after her exhausting day, so I retired to the pagoda, took my vows and received a blessing from U Ba Khin. I sat down on a mat cross-legged in the lotus posture and closed my eyes but without allowing sleep to come. I stayed that way until about three in the morning.

For Eve the days that followed were a refreshing holiday in a beautiful part of the world. The atmosphere was relaxing, there was always the heady scent of flowers in the air and there were kindly, unsophisticated people from many countries to meet and exchange conversation with. There were local beauty-spots to be visited, shops and markets to be gazed at, strange customs to hold her enthralled.

For me those days were all of that and more. I had come with the firm intention to throw out all my preconceived ideas on the course my search should take; I drifted. As the mood took me so I acted. I listened to those who spoke. I sat in on the religious services. I mixed among the people of the center.

I meditated in the little pagoda room every day and at any time I felt like it. I was determined not to be trapped by the intellectual vicious circle which had so impeded my understanding during my last course of study here.

And to my great joy I found that at last my mind could be made quiet.

The experience was deeply fulfilling. I am not sure, even now, whether I can describe it adequately for it is so richly personal that words seem insufficient. It was all that I had expected, yet if I had expected it to be merely self-rewarding, a kind of tonic for a restless mind, I had drastically underestimated it.

There was much much more. The first few days of meditation were difficult for my mind was slow to free itself from the discordant influences of months of active business and social life. But I noticed that deep concentration came more easily and quickly this time than it had previously. In about three days the mind was clear, crystal clear. It was ready to proceed through this complete freedom from all thought to *vipassanā* or insight.

At this stage my teacher instructed me to be aware of the cellular movements and the active, impermanent nature of the body processes. In time, and with a determination not to rush things, I found I could do this. I was told to start at the top of my head and slowly work on down the body to the tips of my toes, applying a truly penetrating concentration to each part on the way.

Gradually I became aware of tingling sensations throughout those parts of my body upon which this intense concentration was focussed. When concentration was directed to my right hand, for instance, I experienced the wild dance of electrons producing a warm glow throughout the hand, and the same effect was achieved on each part of my person in turn.

The effect was remarkable. After a few days of this practice I was fully aware of the true nature of the physical structure of the body as being impermanent and subject to change. I had read about this and I had been told about it. Now I was actually experiencing it for myself. The keen awareness of this molecular motion was beginning to produce a glow of heat—and are we not taught in science that when there is motion there is friction and friction produces heat?

With further contemplation my awareness turned to the impermanent and transitory nature of the perceptions and there was a keen awareness of their rising and passing. I was becoming clearly aware of the oscillating nature of all bodily and physical processes. The concept of anicca was becoming crystal clear and although I had learned of molecular and atomic theories I was now, with the microscope-like eye of a clear mind, actually experiencing the facts that were previously only theories.

Besides experiencing the atomic theories in action in my own body, and as they related to my senses and perceptions, all I had learned of the science of vibration was becoming a conscious part of me. My mind reflected on the various aspects of vibration from subsonic sounds to the sound frequencies, ultrasonic, radio frequencies, very high frequencies, ultra violet, x-rays, cosmic radiations.

My mind was ranging through the whole gamut of vibrations and their speeds and wave lengths, and how they were all part and parcel of every existing thing as well as having an influence on my life. My body was getting warmer during this period. The more I persisted in my meditations the hotter I grew although the temperature in the pagoda remained uniform and moderate. Soon it felt as if it would be consumed with the intense heat that was manifesting itself. In Buddhist terms I knew what was happening: I was repaying my karmic debts for past misdeeds in a concentrated form.

At this point the teacher made me take a vow to remain perfectly still for one hour periods without moving. I was to make no movement of any kind, not even flick an eyebrow. Knowing this would be an extreme test of will I agreed. The heat and pain became intense. The suffering was more than unbearable, it was searing and terrible, but persistence and perseverance had been demanded and

I had agreed to it.

Buddha's teachings on the nature of suffering became clearly experienced through my entire being. It was like fire, burning and scorching. And naturally the desire to be free from the agony was intense also. The slightest movement of the body would bring instant relief, but only for a moment, after which the agony would return when I sat still again.

As the days passed the pain persisted, and as the pain persisted so did my desire to be free from it. But there was to be no relief—perhaps a gradual simmering down, but no relief so long as I desired relief. My mind reflected on anicca again and it occurred to me that if everything was subject to change so was dukkha or suffering. As long as the mind was functioning in its usual egocentric fashion suffering was bound to continue. There was an intense desire to be free from suffering and this very desire was perpetuating the suffering. This must have been the turning point, my moment of truth. Suddenly, at a point of supreme frustration, my mind stopped functioning for it realized it could not bring about a cessation of dukkha. The desire to be free from suffering ceased as the realization occurred that it could not be sought after and brought about. There was an infinitesimal attachment to the self and suddenly, like a bolt of lightning, something snapped and when the search stopped there was relief. It was an extraordinary and, for me, totally unprecedented experience.

"There was an indescribable calm. There was cool equanimity that seemed to fill and encompass entirety. There was everything and nothing, a peace which passes all understanding. The mind and body were transcended. The mind was quiet. It was not pleasure as we understand the word; joy comes nearer to expressing the experience. There are no longer any words to carry on with." These were the sentences I wrote down later in a quite inadequate attempt to record the superb moment of my enlightenment.

I cannot, and never will, lose the memory of that moment. It will always remain absolutely unforgettable and ineradicable in my mind. It was the culmination, rich beyond all my expectations, of the search. It was the fulfillment and justification of all my hopes.

❋

It is useless to try to convey to the reader the full meaning which this strange and truly wonderful experience had for me. A quiet mind is what many yearn for and if I can at least show that this so elusive state is attainable, that the seemingly impossible can be achieved, than I shall have amply succeeded in the purpose of this account.

For me a quiet mind was top priority. The stresses to which my mind had been subjected as an espionage agent living, as he is bound to live, a kind of double life with its frequent incidence of such emotions as anxiety, pain and fear are the stresses everyone experiences but in a concentrated form.

For a spy, one might say, the emotional strains of a lifetime are telescoped into a few short, hectic years. My need for a quiet mind was urgent. But it is no less important for a business executive under pressure or a housewife harassed by an irritable husband or a kitchenfull of screaming kids. The end result is the same and the yearning for release is the same.

For the business tycoon or office worker there is the occasional game of golf, the weekend cottage by the sea or even the blonde friend installed comfortably in an apartment well away from the unsuspecting—or, for that matter, highly suspicious—wife.

For the housewife tied to home by family responsibilities there's the prospect of being taken out to dinner or a dance, a visit to the movies, an amorous adventure with the milkman, the annual holiday with the family.

But all that these diversions offer is a little temporary relaxation, a change of scene. Once they are over and normal routine is re-established the same stresses and strains take over again. We start to look forward to the next holiday, the next trip to the movies, the next round of golf.

My experience of *anicca* which means the change, impermanence, transitoriness of all things, and vipassanā, the understanding of the true nature of self, the awareness of self, was certainly a turning point in my life. I had found what I was looking for, I was, to some extent at least, "enlightened". But as I have already indicated this new and valuable state was not an end in itself.

Perhaps I had expected it to be just that, but having attained it

I then found—and I think half expected this too—that it was only a beginning. Being attuned, switched on, initiated, call it what you will, I now found many further doors opened, leading to a richer life.

One potent force that was awakened in me was the desire to pass on to others what I had learned and share the enjoyment and fulfilment of it. That was undoubtedly the motivation for writing this book about an essentially personal experience.

Before I left the center I had a number of talks with U Ba Khin and I put it to him that, should meditation spread to more people throughout the world, and gain a wider acceptance among different kinds of people there would be a good deal more harmony in international affairs. As things stood, this way of life was followed by an insignificant minority, most of them monks, holymen, gurus, priests and the like. U Ba Khin himself, with his heavy government responsibilities and extraordinarily active life, was merely the exception that proved the truth of this. He smiled broadly.

"It has been my life ambition to teach Buddha-Dhamma in the West," he told me. "After thirty years of research work and trials, with success and failures, I have reached a stage at which I consider myself well qualified to teach the people of the world. I have tried since 1966 to get a passport to go abroad for this very purpose, but there's a ban on the issue of passports except for governmental purposes and for those leaving Burma for good."

I had to admire the old man's energy. At seventy-one he was prepared to leave his native land and set out on a mission whose sole aim would be to help others in foreign countries to achieve a happiness which they didn't even know was possible. He knew the task would be difficult but even in the evening of his life he clearly felt the undertaking worth while.

"Anicca is not reserved for men who have renounced the world for a homeless life; it's for the householder as well," he said. "The world is facing serious problems; it is just the right time for everyone to take to vipassanā meditation and learn how to find a deep pool of quiet in the midst of all that is happening today."

I reminded U Ba Khin that the average Western mind was not receptive to this kind of thinking. To most of us it would not even occur that there existed a plane of intellectual awareness where the kind of peace to be experienced in meditation could be found. Such an idea would be fanciful and preposterous. Buddhism, unfortunately, was not at all that widespread in the West.

"Whether a Buddha has arisen or not," he replied, "the practice of *sīla* and *samādhi* are present in the world of mankind. In fact, they are the common denominators of all religious faiths. Sīla means virtuous living and is the basis for samādhi, which means control of the mind to one-pointedness. And the two are prerequisites for paññā, by which is meant the understanding of anicca, dukkha and anattā through the practice of vipassanā. This understanding can be developed, as in the days of Buddha, by persons who have no book knowledge whatsoever of Buddhism."

He pointed out that, in any case, a mere reading of Buddhist books or an interest in Buddha-Dhamma did not equip a person to understand. My own experience bore this out. It was only through practice and personal experience that one could reach a true understanding of anicca as an ever-changing process within one's very self that one could understand anicca in the way Buddha intended.

"Buddha's advice to monks was that they should try to maintain the awareness of anicca at all times, whether sitting or standing, walking or lying down. The continuity of awareness of anicca, and so of dukkha and anattā, is the secret of success. For us of today it should suffice if we can understand anicca very well.

"This is the age of science. Men today have no utopia; they will accept nothing unless the results are good, concrete, vivid, personal and here and now. With proper teaching there is no doubt whatsoever of the definite results of vipassanā meditation which will keep a person in a state of well-being and happiness for the rest of his life.

"There is no need for him to be activating anicca all the time. It is sufficient to set aside regular periods in the day or night for the purpose and for this time at least keep the mind and attention inside the body and so continuous that no discursive or distracting thoughts can intrude, for these are detrimental to progress."

Perhaps a little further explanation is necessary at this point on exactly what is meant by concentrating the attention on parts of the body. The teaching of Buddha—and this was twenty-five centuries ago—went a stage further than modern atomic theories on the composition of matter. He taught that all matter which exists in the universe, whether animate or inanimate, is composed of particles called *kalāpas* which are very much smaller than atoms. Kalāpas die out as soon as they are created, hence the continuous process of change called anicca.

The actual size of a kalāpa is said by Buddhists to be 1/46656th part of a particle of dust from the wheel of a chariot in summer in India; its life span is a moment, there being a trillion such moments in the wink of an eye. In vipassanā meditation one's concentration has to be directed, as I have described in my own case, on parts of the body but it is not upon anatomical features that the mind dwells. The attention must be focussed inward towards the actual composition of being.

As the attention moves slowly and with utmost concentration from feet to legs to arms to head each bit comes under the most microscopic scrutiny. It is the awareness of the movement and change and friction of the kalāpas which go to make up the body tissue, bones and blood which gives rise to the intense sensation of burning and ultimate transcending of ordinary consciousness.

It is this state which, under U Ba Khin's extraordinary teaching, holds the promise of well-being and lifelong happiness.

Before we took our leave I asked U Ba Khin if there was any way in which his teaching could be brought to the notice of the "outside" world should he be unsuccessful in his attempts to obtain a passport and journey abroad. He was, he told me, considering the idea of authorizing some of his disciples in other countries to conduct Buddhist meditation courses on his behalf. Little did I realize at the time that I would be chosen as one of them.

That night I returned for the last time to the tiny wedge-shaped meditation room in the gold pagoda with which I had become so familiar. I stayed there until nearly three. When I emerged the center was in total darkness under the black Burmese sky from which shone a million bright stars. The only sound was the low murmuring of night insects. The world was asleep.

I made my way to bed, sad at the thought that in only a few hours I should be leaving Rangoon and the oasis of light and peace that surrounded this gentle old man who, with charm, grace and vast good humour, had such a unique capacity for imparting peace of mind to those who sought his teaching.

At 5 a.m. sharp we were awakened and served with a sumptuous breakfast of exotic fruits expertly prepared and served. We dressed hurriedly to catch the plane for Calcutta, where I had arranged to spend a few days with a friend who worked at the German consulate. The entire group at the center were already up and waiting to see us off in the cold morning light. We said our goodbyes all round and rushed off to the airport.

I heard nothing of U Ba Khin until some months after Eve and I had arrived back at our home just outside London. One morning a neatly typed letter was delivered, postmarked Rangoon, and in it U Ba Khin told me I had been selected to give Buddhist-Dhamma instruction to new students on his behalf. He gave me precise guidance on how to go about selecting students and what course of tuition to give them, and his letter went on:

"What is very essential before you make a start in giving the Dhamma is to get yourself 'tuned in' with me in the shrine room of the Center at the fixed hours of 0800 in the morning and 2000 hours in the evening (Burma Standard Time) and then to share what you have got with the students under your charge so that they also get the cover of nibbāna dhātu according to Transformer Theory."

I was puzzled but he went on to explain that he had conducted a number of experiments in giving Dhamma to his disciples abroad by distant control. "The results are wonderful," he wrote. The whole scheme, fantastic though it may sound, was organized in a very business-like way which was typical of U Ba Khin the government official. It was unusual and sensational by any standards.

"There will be regular transmissions of my thought waves charged with *nibbāna dhātu* daily between the hours of 0730 and 0830, and 2000 and 2100 (Burma Standard Time), during which periods you can get yourself very easily 'tuned in' with Burma, Rangoon, International Meditation Center (IMC). Also, there will be special transmissions between the hours of 1930 and 2000 on Tuesdays, Thursdays and Sundays which you can take advantage of if your anicca level is high.

"It is just like the radio world," he went on. "In the same way as a radio for reception must be powerful enough to tune in to the transmission of a particular station at a great distance, so also your power of reception with anicca at its base must be good to be able to "tune in" with the transmission from my shrine room, to which your attention must be directed.

"You are aware that the atmosphere throughout the world is at this time permeated with the forces of evil which stem from *taṇhā, māna* and *diṭṭhi* of the highest order. There must therefore be disturbances and resistances on the way; but my experiments show that the power of transmission from here is strong enough to reach my disciples in any part of the world if only they take the necessary precaution to keep the doors of reception open with the awareness of anicca.

"If you want to make a special arrangement for your own course you will inform me the period available for the purpose and the date from which you want to start *ānāpāna-vipassanā* meditation. Please let me know by return of mail how you feel about the proposed arrangements."

The Author and U Ba Khin at International Meditation Centre

U Ba Khin gave me the addresses of five others who had been authorized to give meditation in the United States, Canada and the Netherlands and to whom he had given particulars of his distant control plan. I was the only person selected in Britain. He cautioned me to forget about money if I was going to give courses. Success depended on the quality of the teaching and not upon any money that came "by stretching out both your hands."

"Perhaps you know that the caretaker work of our center is done by a small group of my devoted disciples from the Accountant General's office. The strictest injunction is for any one of them not to show any signs (not to speak of an appeal) for money required to keep the center going. There is no admission or subscription fee or fixed donation payable... If anyone feels that as a return for the gift of Dhamma he or she should donate some thing in kind or cash there is no objection.

"But we accept aid only from those who have purified themselves with vipassanā meditation under me and not from any other person. Who knows what is their source of income? We take no chances because we want the center to be developed on the foundation of Purity."

I calculated the British equivalents of the Burmese times he had given me (1:30 a.m. and 1:30 p.m.) and meditated at those times on a number of occasions. I found quite genuinely that the "tuning in" procedure worked; I felt waves of strength entering my mind and my being and can certainly vouch for the greater depth of my meditation at the prescribed times than at other times. I felt U Ba Khin had made a discovery to which modern science might with advantage turn its analytical attention.

In spite of U Ba Khin's faith in my ability to pass on to others what I had learned I have not so far gathered meditation students to my home for a course of study and perhaps I never will, for it was soon after my last letter from Rangoon that I was appointed to a security job in the United States and life became hectic for me once again.

That night in the pagoda when the search ended, a search which had led me to many strange and wonderful parts of the world and in which I had directed my inquiries to many unconventional philosophies and diverse practices, was a night which has had far-reaching consequences. I knew a quiet mind at last. I knew the very fact that a quiet mind is attainable, which is a rare sort of knowledge. Maybe I was right when I wrote later, "There are no more words."

18

The Only Antidote to Conflict

ALTHOUGH every human being who has a strong will and an ability to persevere can reach the quiet and peaceful state of nirvana the achievement of it, the devotion and practice, all takes time. And time is the commodity most people are short of these days.

The trial and error, the frustration which arises from initial failure, the constant going back to square one, all make serious inroads into the amount of spare time an average individual can spend on doing something that isn't directly concerned with his work or his home life. Because of social or family duties, economical or professional commitments, it's difficult for most average men and women to give the necessary time to a search for nirvana.

The result is that most people do nothing about it. They put up with strains because they don't see any immediate way out; it is part of living and they just accept it.

But among certain groups, notably artists, students and others for whom time is just as precious, a kind of instant bliss is sought as a peace substitute. They "switch on" with LSD, mescaline and hashish with effects that are so transcendental and out-of-this-world that they tend to go into raptures over what they call "divine," "mystical," and "religious" experiences. And what addicts of these drugs will never accept is that their experiences during "high" moments induced by these artificial means are really nothing more than pathetic self-deception. I located a group of pot smokers in London (some were on other drugs) and they described their experiences to me.

"I was filled with love," said a pale, thin slip of a girl with long, blonde hair lying around her small shoulders. "There was a light that was both God and the sun," said a gaunt young man. A shock-haired youth rhapsodized: "There came a knowledge beyond all doubts, and convictions, tenacious in their strength, as if LSD had opened a curtain and allowed the light of wisdom to shine through."

The youngsters cooperated with me willingly and were only too glad to talk to someone who was prepared to listen to their wonderful reports. Other comments I got were: "I was overwhelmed with feelings of forgiveness, compassion, love and other such emotions." "I saw God as part of myself; I was God." "My entire being was filled with an indescribable ecstasy." "I knew God permeated every crevice of the universe. Every space, no matter how small was filled with His love, every wall was pierced no matter how thick and He surrounded every human being."

A serious young man with a strong Northern accent told me: "It became a reality that to find God we only had to look within ourselves and everywhere around us." I assumed he was speaking for the group and not only for himself.

Various people have experimented with LSD and described the intoxicating effects of this and other similar drugs. But the inadequacy of language to fully relate them and the great spectrum of human feelings which seem to lack clearly defined boundaries make it difficult to draw comparisons.

In a carefully controlled medical experiment LSD was administered to me. I wished to investigate reports of its mystic-like phenomena and to satisfy my curiosity about its dubious value in comparison with the rich and fulfilling nirvana that I knew

I decided that, like hypnosis, the states brought on by such means differ from the truly mystical nirvana in three major respects: their sudden onset, relatively brief duration and, most marked of all, the complete absence of any lasting influence upon the personality or insight into the laws of life. It is true that in the ecstasy of the moment all else is either forgotten or seems unimportant or unreal, but wisdom and understanding is displaced.

It appears from some reports that the taking of LSD does seem to produce an authentic mystical state sometimes. But the disadvantage that no real and permanent transformation occurs in the personality seems to me an overriding one.

There is no residue of insight left behind to induce a quiet mind in the subject, who must then wait, and in many sad cases crave, for the next "shot". The best this drug can do is offer a quick, unsatisfactory glimpse of something which can be experienced through the truly religious manifestation of enlightenment.

So far as my own researches were concerned I concluded that drugs are no substitute for the arduous process of true meditation in the search for a quiet mind for they do not bring about the necessary and lasting personality changes. They are more likely to weaken the will than strengthen it.

This is not to imply that LSD and related drugs do not have useful psychotherapeutic value. There are cases which have produced valuable psychological insights and facilitated personality growth. But this growth takes place only if the patient is intellectually and emotionally prepared to cope, understand and make use of the insight obtained.

Recent electroencephalographic studies have been made in India and Japan on yogis and Zen practitioners who have experienced *satori* or Zen enlightenment and as these subjects approached the state of ecstasy or enlightenment their alpha rhythms became transformed into a pattern similar to a pattern preceding REM (rapid eye movement) sleep and dream sleep or intense waking concentration.

Buddhists usually attain enlightenment by long and disciplined meditation, fixing their eyes on one position and practising rhythmic breathing. This process usually takes years of devoted application before proficiency is attained. They may seem to be asleep, but in fact they are balanced delicately between relaxed serenity and instant alertness. My story of Dr. Suzuki in an earlier chapter is an example of this state.

Studies have been conducted in the United States to determine if a subject could be trained to bring on this state through the use of a feedback system in which an electrical filter was attached to the electroencephalograph machine and set to the individual's particular alpha wave frequency. At the moment alpha began a switch would flip automatically to ring a bell which thereby alerted the subject that he was in the state.

As a result of these experiments the electroencephalograph, ordinarily used as a detector device, was now being employed successfully to teach by giving feedback. After a few sessions volunteers were learning to identify what usually takes years of patient training and hard work to accomplish. In Zen practice, continual meditation should finally lead to an experience of transcendence, a union with the unconscious and an illumination of one's physical self in unity with all nature.

Scientific studies of meditation are being carried out by the physiology department of the All-India Institute of Medical Sciences in Delhi. Professor B. K. Anand and Dr. G. S. Chhina claim they have found scientific evidence to substantiate some of the claims of Indian mystics. Electrocardiograph charts made while yogis were in a state of trance show that volunteers were able to slow their heartbeat and pulse rates to a mere flutter.

The institute found evidence to explain how some mystics can be buried alive for long periods. While in a trance these rare individuals were able to reduce their body oxygen requirements to 50 per cent of the amount needed by a normal person at rest. Dr. Chhina states that the yogis achieve an advanced state of alpha rhythm activity and are capable of conditioning the central nervous system to disregard outside disturbances when they concentrate on a small area of interest.

Does all this have a connection with the state of reality experienced in meditation to the point of nirvana? What have these unnatural interferences with the normal workings of the mind to do with the state of reality, love and enlightenment which, as I have proved, we have to realize by ourselves and through ourselves if we are to find true peace and joy?

As with drugs, the learning to control the alpha state by artificial inducements does not produce the necessary insight and experience of self to go beyond the process of duality, enter enlightenment and end suffering. Certainly not on the strength of the scientific experiments so far conducted, anyway. And what developments there have been in this direction will be a long time becoming available to any but laboratory subjects.

We can therefore proceed into the fascinating study of transcendental meditation by using the means one has at hand. As humans we all suffer, some more than others. We are in constant conflict from birth to death. At birth a baby has to yell to get air into its tiny lungs; it feels cold and yells again. It weeps with pitiful intensity for food to fill its empty belly. Then, inevitably, a rattle, perhaps with bells attached, comes on the scene to startle the infant and jar its nerves. Surprises like this induce a comfortable chortle when the baby has got used to the fact that the initial uncertainty and fear brought about by the sudden noise are not necessarily the prelude to a disaster.

It's all part of growing up, and if baby imagines that things will get easier for him as he grows older he is surely in for another surprise. Life is conflict. As a child grows his potential for conflict increases in proportion to the number of new people he encounters and the experiences he has.

He is in constant conflict with his parents, his brothers and sisters, his school teachers, the activities he takes part in and the work expected of him. And he often finds he is in conflict with himself.

In adulthood there are the conflicts of work and social activities, courtship, love, marriage and parenthood. There is conflict at every turn and we call up the human qualities of perseverance, determination and forbearance to combat it. We spend most of our life trying to evade the fact of our conflict by means of the easily available antidotes of entertainments, drink, food, sex, reading, talking, watching TV, going to the movies, dropping out, starting revolutions.

When these get out of hand and become conflicts in themselves we find further antidotes. If drinking or smoking become a problem we vow to give them up, and the giving up, while being an antidote involving the positive action of willpower becomes in itself another conflict. A fat girl with a passion for cream cakes goes on a diet and achieves a slim waistline which is the admiration of all her friends, but only at the expense of the thing she desires most in the world—a cream cake.

The word "painstaking" has about it an aura of well-deserved achievement and rightly so. The gaining of an outstanding honour often involves pain, hard labour either mental or physical, hours of patient and intensive study or application of oneself in some way, all of which is a form of conflict and in which there is a degree of suffering.

What about the person who never does anything more painstaking than plan a robbery so that he has no need to work, or concocts a lie to get himself out of trouble? There is conflict in store for both offenses. The first in an unpleasant encounter with the law or the expectation of it, the second from an uneasy conscience or shame if the lie is found out.

I am not saying, of course, that the diversions man has devised to lessen the conflicts of life are misguided or wrong. Entertainments, in whatever form one cares to take them, are necessary and indeed vital to happiness in the ordinary sense of the word. Both the body and the mind need rest and the batteries have to be recharged some way. But the conventional methods for reviving ourselves in the midst of life's conflicts only partially do the job. They fall short of showing us the true nature of reality. The entertainments and antidotes I mentioned have a proper place in modern life but they do not aid the discovery of a quiet mind.

Where, then, do we go from here? For me the answer to that question lies in my knowledge gained from the rich experience of knowing a quiet mind. I have been helped in the attainment of this knowledge by listening to and understanding the many wise men I have been lucky enough to meet, and by watching them and learning from their example.

I know now that it is not necessary to travel the world in search of a leader or a system for the answers are all within us. In fact such a search is in itself a distraction and only serves to delay the moment of vision. It was only when my search ended that peace followed.

The key is in suffering and conflict; it is necessary to regard the suffering of others with compassion and our own with tolerance and equanimity. We must be aware of it, but silently, without trying to invite this silence by conscious effort. And this silent awareness must be allowed to come about in its own time, anything we do to hasten it merely adds further conflict.

One must be aware of the moment without any attempt to change it; it will change itself. One must be attentive to an extreme degree as often as possible. Even to be attentive that one is not attentive is a form of attentiveness. To know reality one cannot stand outside of it and intellectualize about it, one must enter into it, become it and experience it. Then the mind becomes quiet, at peace with itself.

The beauty of living and the beauty of the earth unfolds and one's actions are no longer self-centered and destructive. Every action becomes creative. The fire of discontent changes from a destructive force consuming our lives into a bright luminous light that fills our lives with peace and joy.

Suffering can be extinguished by accepting that pain is subject to the law of anicca or change as all things are. Try to escape from it and we only nourish it. To know there is no escape frees the mind of its desire to escape. When the mind makes no effort to escape from pain and ceases all resistance it will absorb the pain so that the pain dwindles and gradually becomes imperceptible. Pleasure and pain become one; pain to most of us is, in any case, a form of pleasure for it keeps us occupied in escaping from it.

When we see clearly that suffering is caused by desire, the desire for pleasure or the desire to be free from pain—even the desire to be free from desire—there is no longer the conflict of duality. The observer becomes the observed, the illusion of a separate self disappears, there is integration with the universe. The experience is all. There is no experience of "you" experiencing the experience. There is pure action without purpose, there is love.

Then only can man live dynamically and creatively in peace with himself and therefore with others. He has discovered the quiet mind.

19

The Quiet Mind—A Postscript

MY pursuit of what I termed a "quiet mind" sprang initially from the hectic life I had been leading in my career with United States Intelligence. Serving in the Far East gave me a unique opportunity to experience at close quarters the calming effects of Eastern cultures, so elusive in Western civilization, and this became the starting point for my quest. For someone who had followed my demanding line of work for several years the need to slow down and experience a gentler, more peaceful, way of life was an urgent one and, as the reader will have seen, my investigations bore fruit. I was now relaxed and settled in England with a loving wife and ambitions to raise a family. I thought no more about fulfilling my Burmese teacher U Ba Khin's wish that I should pass on to others what I had learned in the pagoda in Rangoon.

However, day-to-day living brings with it expenses which have to be met and I was soon drawn back into security work. With the manuscript of *The Quiet Mind* safely in the hands of the publisher, I accepted a job in Midwestern America. It was a big mistake! My lifestyle of cultivated calm turned a spectacular somersault as I plunged back into the kind of work from which I thought I had successfully escaped. I soon realized that I was not going to be comfortable in this line of work and that Wisconsin and I would have to part company.

Moreover, Eve and I were planning to have another child. We both knew that she would prefer to be back in England under the care of the national health service. She would have access to the various specialists required to attend to any gynecological surprises and enjoy the excellent antenatal, maternity and postnatal care provided by the service. I resigned from my job, we caught the plane to London, Eve became pregnant and was promptly told by her consultant that if she was to avoid serious problems this time she would have to remain in bed for the entire nine months of the pregnancy.

So began one of the most difficult periods of our lives. If ever I needed a quiet mind it was in the months that followed. Eve did as she was told and took to her bed. I landed a low-paying job with a small local electronics firm testing printed circuit boards from eight in the morning until five at night. The work was tedious but at least it did not have the atmosphere of paranoia associated with security work. We carried on with hopes for a brighter future. The relative stability of this domestic scene was not to survive undisturbed for long, however. Nor was the teaching of meditation to continue to take such a back seat in my life. Some time before this, events in Burma had undergone a major political upheaval. The socialist government of U Nu was toppled in a military coup with far-reaching effects on everyday life. One consequence of the new regime's policies was the forced repatriation to India of all Burmese residents of Indian extraction, together with confiscation by the state of all property and businesses owned by them. One casualty of the new law was a wealthy businessman by the name of S. N. Goenka who, although Burmese by birth, was the son of Indian parents. He had created and built up over the years a prosperous and successful textile business. Now, with time on his hands following the nationalization of his assets and before moving to India, Goenka became a frequent visitor to U Ba Khin's meditation center where he participated in courses and eventually received authorization to teach. I met him briefly during one of my visits and our meeting was to have unforeseen repercussions later.

When Goenka arrived in India in 1969, he arranged a small meditation course for his ageing mother. Other members of the family and a few close friends attended, too, and the course was an immediate success. Goenka's reputation began to spread and he was asked to teach more courses which grew in size and frequency until his students were renting schools and even hotels to accommodate the crowds flocking to hear him speak and to learn Vipassanā.

Goenka's early fame coincided with the height of the hippy movement and flower power during the late 1960s and early 1970s. Thousands of hippies were pouring into India from all parts of the world seeking spiritual understanding and many of them found their way to Goenka's meditation courses. They were obviously delighted with his enlightened teaching and, inevitably, the question arose "Why was it necessary to travel all the way to India for the course?" A demand arose for sessions to be set up in Europe, America and Australia and in other countries where the pace of modern life was taking its toll.

At this point Goenka remembered the young American now living "somewhere in England" whom he had met at the meditation center in Rangoon and who, like himself, was authorized to teach meditation on U Ba Khin's behalf and under his guidance. We had lost contact with each other but he recalled my name and this was enough to steer many of the students in my direction. I must say that at the time they were not entirely welcome; I was preoccupied with increasing the size of my family, tending to Eve's needs and scraping out a living. Suddenly, it seemed that the Coleman residence was being inundated with telegrams, telephone calls and letters demanding that I should begin to teach meditation courses. Frequent callers began to appear on the doorstep, many of them barefoot, dressed in white robes and adorned with flowers, colored beads and other ornaments, all demanding that Mr. Coleman should teach a course in meditation. Clearly, something had to be done to make the situation more tolerable. Finally, I told them that I would run a course provided they stopped coming to the house. To my relief they agreed and departed.

The students set about organizing accommodation at a Presbyterian retreat in Yorkshire, some 250 miles away in the north of England. Life in our street resumed its normal suburban calm—I think the neighbors were quite relieved—and we sat back to await the birth of our child. But as the date set for the course approached I began to wish that Goenka's memory had not been so sharp. It was years since I had taken a meditation course and, to my consternation, I found that I had completely forgotten how to go about it. It was not simply a matter of adopting the lotus position, humming a mantra and hoping for the best: there was a lot more to achieving nibbāna than that. Two days before the course was scheduled to start Eve went into labour, two months earlier than expected, and was rushed into hospital where Mark was born, a breech baby helped into the world by forceps and suffering from jaundice. We were together for just two days before I had to fulfill my promise in Yorkshire. Had I not done so I knew that back home we would have been faced with a further invasion, this time no doubt a very angry one. Eve saw the dire possibility and agreed that this was the sensible solution.

Throughout the years teachers have established their own individual procedures and formats for conducting courses, some more sophisticated than others. I preferred a less structured approach with organizational, administrative and teaching activities being more or less voluntary and each course existing as a self-sufficient entity. What this approach lacked in efficiency it made up for in reduced bureaucracy. Thus the costs of running a course, generally held in rented accommodation, were shared by the students attending. Buddhist teachings are generally given freely to those who ask.

In Yorkshire about forty students were waiting for me when I arrived at the retreat, forty young men and women all anxious to hear how U Ba Khin's meditation teaching would help to refresh their minds, clear them of accumulated clutter and debris and show them the path to self-awareness and peace. My mind was back in the hospital with Eve and our new son as I tried to remember precisely how to begin the course, and how to carry on. However, with introductions over, day one seemed to go well. The second day was easier and the next better still. The students were satisfied and grateful and their pleasure at the progress of the teaching was a joy to see. At the end of the ten-day course I had forty happy hippies on my hands—and furthermore they wanted to know when and where my next course would be held.

By the time I returned home, Eve and Mark were back from hospital and recovering well from their ordeals. With Clark, our first-born, and Dad in the house once again the family reunion was complete. I was soon to find, however, that the Yorkshire air had set off a momentum that was going to be hard to control. That first course was followed shortly after by a further course, then another and another in quick succession. At first most of the courses were taught in England but it wasn't long before I was being invited to teach courses in France, Switzerland, Holland, Belgium, Germany, Denmark, Sweden, Italy and Austria. Soon courses were organized in the East, Midwest and Western United States and Canada and their popularity just seemed to go on escalating. South America, Japan, New Zealand, Australia, Singapore, Thailand, India and Israel all placed themselves on my ever-expanding agenda. There was a waiting list of students in almost every country eager to discover the secrets of the quiet mind.

Since that first course for a group of hippies in Yorkshire in the early 1970s I have conducted hundreds of courses worldwide and taught thousands of students. With advancing years such a hectic schedule could not go on indefinitely and the time eventually came when I needed to slow down and settle for a calmer lifestyle; this realization itself seemed to recall the very beginnings of my interest in the subject. Today, I limit myself to teaching a few courses in Europe and Thailand each year. And I have enjoyed the pleasure of seeing my family grow up—with, I hope, quiet minds.

THERAVĀDA BUDDHISM—THE FIRST 2,500 YEARS

It has long been predicted in Burma and throughout the Buddhist world that the life span of Gotama Buddha's teaching would be 5,000 years. After that span of time the *Dhamma*, the moral law that leads devout Buddhists to the achievement of *nibbāna*, would be lost to the world until such time as it would be rediscovered by the next Buddha, Metteyya. The first half of the Buddha's teaching, up to the 2,500th year, ended in 1956 and it is interesting to trace its evolution. The whole era fell into five periods, each of 500 years, during which the approach to Buddhism and the methods by which it was taught and practised, went through significant changes.

Here is how Buddhists characterize the five periods:

PERIOD ONE

In the 500 years immediately following the Buddha's death the emphasis was on the practice and teaching of meditation. This was known as the Age of Deliverance.

PERIOD TWO

The Age of Concentration followed: here the emphasis was on devotional activities, the building of temples, images, praying, chanting, the lighting of candles and burning of incense. There was practically no meditation.

PERIOD THREE

Then came the Age of Morality or sīla when faithful lay people focused on five, eight or eleven moral precepts while monks were observing no fewer than 227 precepts. Again there was practically no meditation.

Period Four

The Age of Learning saw a shift to intellectual activities. In this period there were great scholastic accomplishments but very little meditation.

Period Five

The Age of Generosity (dāna) superseded the intellectual period and was marked by the philosophy of acquiring merits through kindness to others.

I first visited Thailand in 1954, two years before the end of the 500-year dāna period, and so saw something of the generosity at first hand. It made a profound impression on me at the time. I found that the Thai people I met couldn't do enough to serve or please others. They felt that by doing good deeds they would acquire merits and the accumulation of these merits would bring them closer to salvation. There was an amusing, if slightly disconcerting, side to the examples of generosity that I experienced. Thais seldom missed an opportunity to be helpful and I soon learned to be cautious. You might meet a Thai friend who was wearing a beautiful necktie. If you admired the necktie by saying how nice it looked, off it would come; it would be thrust into your hands as a gift. The same reaction would even occur with an expensive wristwatch or jewelry.

There was another side to the coin, which I found just as disconcerting at first. If I did a favour or some act of kindness for a Thai I might notice that he did not thank me or smile or show any appreciation. After going out of my way to be helpful and getting no sign that my action was appreciated I mistakenly began to feel that the Thais were a surly, ungracious race with no manners. It took me a little while to understand the real reason: that when you did him a kindness a Thai would be anxious, in return, that you should receive all the merits your action deserved. Since the accumulation of merits would contribute to your spiritual development, any expression of appreciation or thanks by him would detract from the amount of merits due for your kindness. Even a polite smile was enough to affect your score of merits. Nevertheless, while I found Thai generosity admirable I felt that their practice of the faith principally through kindness and generosity to be somewhat superficial when compared to the practice of meditation.

The first half of the predicted 5,000 years of the Buddha's teaching came to an end in 1956 and it is expected that the second half, the next 2,500 years or so, will follow the same pattern passing through similar 500 year divisions. The first of these, being experienced now, is known as the *Vimutti* period, or Age of Deliverance, during which the practice of meditation is returning to prominence, as it did in the 500 years immediately following the Buddha Gotama's death.

In 1956 the practice of meditation was conspicuous by its absence. I had developed a keen interest in Buddhism and read everything I could get my hands on. Much of what I read included descriptions and discussions on meditation and it seemed to me that meditation lay at the heart of Buddhist teaching. I realized that to understand Buddhism thoroughly I would have to learn to meditate. I began to look for a teacher. I approached numerous monks at various temples. No one was teaching meditation—no one for that matter was showing much interest at all in the subject. I made enquiries at the larger universities, including the Buddhist University, to no avail. Those I spoke to knew about meditation through their knowledge of the texts, but no one seemed to be interested enough to practise it. I could find no evidence of meditation activities among any of the students or student organizations. It was disappointing, discouraging and frustrating to be in a Buddhist country and yet not be able to learn more about meditation.

At one point I sensed a breakthrough. I heard of a monk in a temple located 100 kilometers away from Bangkok. I got in my car and drove the distance. The monk, when I found him, informed me that he was indeed teaching meditation but only to other monks; he would not teach a layperson. However, a few months later, shortly before I had to return to Washington, I heard of a monk in Bangkok's Wat Mahatai temple who was teaching meditation. I went to him and he agreed to teach me. For a few days I followed his instruction. At last I had found someone who could share with me one of the central and fundamental mysteries of Buddhism.

By this time we had entered into the 2,500th year of the Buddha's teaching. Now, with the second half of the 5,000 year period about to start, the predicted change of direction was indeed becoming apparent. Throughout Thailand and the rest of the Buddhist world vast celebrations were being held to mark the turning point in the Buddhist calendar In Bangkok the huge parade grounds around the old royal palace were packed with a multitude of exhibitions demonstrating aspects of Buddhist life and history. The city bubbled with excitement and the party mood was evident everywhere. The change of direction, the shift from the dāna period of generosity to a revival of the Age of Deliverance, the Vimutti period, was beginning.

As it happened, I had accumulated several weeks of unused holiday entitlement and on my return trip to Washington decided to stop off in Burma where, I was told, there were now a number of centers teaching meditation. Courses were even available in English, since Burma was a former colony of Great Britain. At the Strand Hotel in Rangoon I was directed to U Ba Khin's center where I was accepted to undertake a course.

U BA KHIN—HIS LIFE AND HIS MISSION

There was a famous scholar monk by the name of Ledi Sayadaw (1846-1923) living in Burma who broke with the tradition of restricting his teaching to other monks and agreed to teach lay people. He selected three people as his first lay students, one of them a wealthy farmer named Saya Thet (1873-1945). Ledi Sayadaw was so pleased with Saya Thet's progress that he authorized him to teach meditation to other lay people. Saya Thet returned to his farm and began to organize courses for small groups. His fame soon spread.

In the government accountant general's office a new employee, a young accountant named U Ba Khin (1899-1971), had been in his post for just a few days when he heard of Saya Thet's teaching. He made up his mind to attend one of the scheduled courses. To take ten days' leave so soon after starting his job was out of the question, but the urge to go was strong. U Ba Khin decided to disregard his boss's objections and attend the course, fully realizing that he risked getting the sack on his return. In fact, when he returned to his desk after the course a large white envelope was waiting for him. Expecting that the letter would contain his dismissal, U Ba Khin was surprised, and delighted, to find that during his absence he had been promoted to chief of his section. The incident proved to be not only the start of a distinguished career, during which he rose to become Accountant General himself, but also the beginning of his lifetime mission to spread throughout the world the deepest teachings of Buddhism through meditation.

One early assignment took U Ba Khin on a journey that he was unlikely ever to forget. He was ordered to travel throughout the entire country to conduct audits at every railway depot. In the north of the country he visited a depot situated not very far from the monastery of a celebrated monk by the name of Webu Sayadaw, who most Burmese believed to be an *arahant* or fully enlightened person. He was held in high regard throughout the country. U Ba Khin decided to pay his respects to Webu Sayadaw and, being unfamiliar with the area, asked a railway clerk to accompany him and act as his guide through the forest paths. After a long and arduous journey they arrived at the monastery gates to be met by a nun in white robes who refused to let them see the venerable monk. "You should have made an appointment months ago," she said. U Ba Khin explained that he did not know he was going to be in the area until a short while ago. The nun eventually allowed the two to enter, but warned them that Webu Sayadaw was engaged in meditating in his straw hut and must not be disturbed.

Paying respects to a monk is usually done by squatting on the ground with hands folded in front and bowing three times. U Ba Khin assured the nun that this was all he intended and it would not interrupt the monk's meditation. The straw hut or cabin was elevated off the ground by four logs to keep insects and animals from entering. U Ba Khin squatted down in front of it and bowed three times in respect. Suddenly the door of the hut opened and a black cloud of mosquitoes flew out revealing Webu Sayadaw sitting there in the lotus posture in his yellow robes; he was looking down at U Ba Khin paying his respects.

"Who are you?" he asked.

"I am U Ba Khin."

"What is your aspiration?"

"Nibbāna," replied U Ba Khin.

"How do you expect to find nibbāna?" asked the monk.

"Through the awareness of anicca."

Webu Sayadaw was surprised. "Where did you learn about this?" he asked.

"Through my teacher Saya Thet, the wealthy farmer."

"Then you must start teaching right away so that others can benefit from what you have learned," said Webu Sayadaw.

Through this brief exchange Webu Sayadaw had evidently recognized in U Ba Khin one who had achieved the rare state of awareness. According to the Buddha everything that exists has three essential characteristics—anicca, dukkha and anattā: impermanence, unsatisfactoriness and egolessness. It is because of our lack of real understanding of these characteristics that we have cravings and aversions and consequently suffering. The practice of Vipassanā meditation provides us with the actual experience and understanding of these characteristics and consequently an end to delusion, cravings and aversions, and suffering, in other words nibbāna.

The door of the cabin closed as suddenly as it had opened and U Ba Khin bowed again three times in respect. Having been ordered to begin teaching without delay he looked around for his first student. The railway clerk, waiting to take the visiting accountant back through the forest, was leaning against a coconut tree smoking a cheroot, a Burmese cigar. U Ba Khin called him over and, finding a suitably quiet spot for the purpose, began teaching him meditation. U Ba Khin's mission had taken off and its effects were to be felt throughout the world in the years that followed.

He conducted his first formal meditation course some years later in his government office after he was promoted to Accountant General, having obtained permission to do so from the Prime Minister. There were about fourteen students, most of them members of the Accountant General's staff. In due course a property was acquired in the suburbs of Rangoon and a meditation center established. U Ba Khin conducted courses there until his death. Today, practically every temple in Burma and other Buddhist countries provides meditation courses and many new temples have been established exclusively for the purpose. Every university, college and secondary school has a meditation group or society. Meditation is even taught in kindergartens.

But U Ba Khin was never able to fulfill personally his dearest wish, to travel abroad to reach new audiences. The political climate made it impossible for him to obtain a passport or exit visa to leave Burma. It was not until after his death in 1971 that his aspiration that the Dhamma spread to the West was realized.

S.N. Goenka continued to teach Westerners as well as Indians in his courses all over India, and in 1979 began to travel to other parts of the world to teach as well. Centers began to be established in many countries until today there are more than seventy centers worldwide teaching meditation in the tradition of U Ba Khin as taught by Goenka.

U Ba Khin's two closest Burmese disciples, Sayama and U Chit Tin, were given permission to leave the country in 1978 and they pursued a vigorous campaign to spread the teaching. Today there are meditation groups and centers in many non-Buddhist parts of the world with hundreds of teachers conducting courses. Western audiences are among the strongest participants. In July 1999 an ordination course under the sponsorship of Sayama and U Chit Tin was held at the International Meditation Center in the U.K. when over a period of ten days 120 students were ordained as Buddhist monks.

Thousands of other lay students in the West have been introduced to the basic tenets of the Buddha's teaching by numerous Western teachers who were introduced to the Mahasi Sayadaw method of meditation during their travels in Asia during the 1960s and 1970s. In more recent years some of the Burmese monks have also been able to travel out and teach in the west as well.

And so the growth of interest in spiritual development has proceeded apace. One result of the Chinese occupation of Tibet was that large numbers of lamas, including the Dalai Lama, were thrown into exile to relocate themselves in India and in western locations. They promptly established religious centers and centers for meditation in order to cater to the spiritual development of large numbers of people. Great Britain has seen a surge of interest no less remarkable. In the 1970s a renowned Thai monk named Ajahn Chaa, of the forest meditation tradition, visited England and along with his disciple Ajahn Sumedho set up the Amaravati Buddhist Monastery and the Chithurst Buddhist Monastery in West Sussex in the south of England. Under the guidance of Ajahn Sumedho the facilities at these centers, and associated facilities, have been used for the training and ordination of the *Sangha* of monks as well as offering training in meditation and the Buddhist way of life to a large number of lay people. And of course with the rapid advance of information technology a considerable amount of information on meditation can be found on the Internet.

When I set out on my researches in Thailand, a Buddhist

country, in 1954 it was almost impossible to find anyone involved in meditation. By 1957 I had met my first teacher, a monk at a Bangkok monastery, and shortly after that I was privileged to meet U Ba Khin and to receive teaching from him, subsequently gaining his authority to pass on to others what I had learned. In 1971, living in England and forced through circumstances to take a job in the United States, I had doubts that I would ever be able to fulfill his wish that I should teach others the Dhamma. Today, such is the interest generated over the years, I have no doubt that during my last breath I will still be teaching Dhamma.

Shortly before he died U Ba, Khin made this pronouncement:

> The time clock of Vipassanā has now struck—that is, for the revival of the Buddha-Dhamma, Vipassanā in practice. We have no doubt whatsoever about definite results accruing to those who would with open mind sincerely undergo a course of training under a competent teacher. I mean results which will be accepted as good, concrete, vivid, personal, here and now: results which will keep them in good stead and in a state of well-being and happiness for the rest of their lives. May all beings be happy and may peace prevail in the world.

Glossary

Ānāpāna respiration, the meditation practice of the awareness of respiration.

Ajahn (Thai) teacher.

Anattā non-self, egoless, without essence, without substance. One of the three basic characteristics. See also **anicca, dukkha.**

Anicca impermanent, ephemeral, changing. One of the three basic characteristics. See also **anattā, dukkha.**

Arahant liberated being; one who has destroyed all his mental impurities. See **Buddha.**

Bhikkhu (Buddhist) monk; meditator. Feminine form bhikkhunī: nun.

Buddha enlightened person; one who has discovered the way to liberation, has practised it, and has reached the goal by his own efforts. The historical Buddha, Gotama, was born and lived in the fifth century B.C. in Northern India.

Chakra circle, wheel, psychic centers in the human body.

Dāna charity, generosity, donation.

Dhamma phenomenon; object of mind; nature; natural law; law of liberation, i.e. teaching of an enlightened person.

Dhātu element, natural condition, property.

Diṭṭhi view, belief, dogma, theory, esp. false theory, ungrounded opinion.

Dukkha suffering, unsatisfactoriness. One of the three basic characteristics. See also **anattā, anicca.**

Gita abbr. for Bhagavad Gita, the dialogues between Krishna and Arjuna; the most popular and best known of all the sacred scriptures from ancient India.

Kalāpa smallest indivisible unit of matter, composed of the four elements and their characteristics.

Kamma action, specifically an action performed by oneself that will have an effect on one's future.

Karma (Sanskrit) see **Kamma.**

Koan "riddles" used in the teaching of Zen Buddhism to help the student realize satori (enlightenment).

Kwannon the Japanese goddess of mercy, represented with many hands, typifying generosity and kindness.

Lama name for Tibetan Buddhist monks, meaning 'great master'.

Lamaism another name for Tibetan Buddhism.

Linga Hindu symbol for the male creative power; a manifestation of the god Shiva. See yoni.

Longyi Burmese wrap-around tube skirt, worn by both sexes.

Māna pride, conceit, arrogance.

Mani (Tibetan) jewel, symbolizing the factors of method, the altruistic intention to become enlightened; compassion and love.

Mantra in Hinduism and Buddhism, a sacred utterance (syllable, word, or verse) that is thought to possess spiritual or mystical power.

Mazuna Japanese lettuce or mustard.

Mudra (Sanskrit) seal, sign, a gesture or position, usually of the hand, used in meditation.

Nibbāna the extinction of the flames of greed, hatred, and delusion.; freedom from suffering; the ultimate reality; the unconditioned. (Sanskrit: **nirvāṇa**).

Nirvana (Sanskrit) see **nibbāna**

Om (Sanskrit) a sacred syllable, or sound of numinous power, chanted for concentration and spiritual benefit.

Pāli line; text; the texts recording the teaching of the Buddha; hence language of these texts. Historical, linguistic, and archaeological evidence indicates that this was a language actually spoken in northern India at or near the time of the Buddha. At a later date the texts were translated into Sanskrit, which was exclusively a literary language.

Paññā wisdom. The third of the three trainings by which the Noble Eightfold Path is practised. See also **sīla, samādhi**.

Sīla morality; abstaining from physical and vocal actions that cause harm to oneself and others. The first of the three trainings by which the Noble Eightfold Path is practised. See also **paññā, samādhi**.

Sadhu Indian ascetic.

Samādhi concentration, control of one's own mind. The second of the three trainings by which the Noble Eightfold Path is practised. See also **paññā, sīla**.

Sangha congregation; community of ariyā, i.e. those who have experienced nibbāna; community of Buddhist monks or nuns.

Satori sudden enlightenment, in the Zen Buddhist tradition.

Sayadaw (Burmese) noble or venerable teacher, title applied to monks

Sayagyi (Burmese) dear or beloved teacher.

Shakti Hindu god, as the wife of Shiva, the female principle; see **Shiva**.

Shiva Hindu god, husband of Shakti, the male principle; see **Shakti**.

Stupa hemispherical commemorative monument usually housing sacred relics associated with the Buddha or other saintly persons.

Sutra discourse of the Buddha or one of his leading disciples.

Tantra Hindu and Buddhist systems of esoteric practices used for both the attainment of spiritual experiences and the fulfillment of worldly desires.

Taṇhā literally, 'thirst'. Includes both craving and its opposite, aversion. The Buddha identified taṇhā as the cause of suffering.

Tara Buddhist saviour/goddess with several forms, popular in Nepal, Tibet, and Mongolia.

Theravāda literally, 'teaching of the elders'. The teachings of the Buddha, in the form in which they have been preserved in the countries of south Asia (Burma, Sri Lanka, Thailand, Laos, Cambodia). Generally recognized as the oldest form of the Buddha's teachings.

Vajra (Sanskrit) thunderbolt, diamond. Tibetan ritual object used in Tibetan Buddhist ceremonies.

Vedantic of the Vedanta school, one of the orthodox schools of Indian philosophy, forming the basis of most modern schools of Hinduism.

Vimutti release, deliverance, emancipation.

Vipassanā introspection, insight which purifies the mind; specifically insight into the impermanent, suffering, and egoless nature of the mental-physical structure.

Wat Thai temple.

Yin-yang (Japanese thought) two opposing yet complementary forces, or principles, that making up all phenomena. Yin is earth, female, dark, passive. Yang is heaven, male, light, active.

Yoni the Hindu symbol for the female sexual organ, and symbol of the goddess Shakti, consort of Shiva. See **linga**.

Zazen Zen Buddhist sitting meditation; characteristic of the Soto sect

Zendo Zen Buddhist meditation room or hall, where zazen and other practices are observed.

About Pariyatti

Pariyatti is dedicated to providing affordable access to authentic teachings of the Buddha about Dhamma theory *(pariyatti)* and practice *(paṭipatti)* of Vipassana meditation. A nonprofit 501(c)(3) organization since 2002, Pariyatti is sustained by contributions from individuals who appreciate and want to share the incalcuable value of the Dhamma teachings. We invite you to visit www.pariyatti.org to learn more about our programs, services, resources and ways to support publishing and other undertakings.

Selected works published by Pariyatti:

Meditation Now, S.N. Goenka

Karma and Chaos: New and Collected Essays on Vipassana Meditation, Paul R. Fleischman, M.D.

Cultivating Inner Peace, Paul R. Fleischman, M.D.

The Vision of Dhamma: Buddhist Writings of Nyanaponika Thera, Bhikkhu Bodhi

Along the Path: The Meditator's Companion to the Buddha's Land, Kory Goldberg and Michelle Décary

The Noble Eightfold Path: Way to the End of Suffering, Bhikkhu Bodhi

The Life of the Buddha: According to the Pali Canon, Bhikkhu Ñāṇamoli

Available at bookstores or online at www.Pariyatti.org